AF481081

MY BIG EGO

A Practical Guide to Shifting from Fear to Love

Vanessa Wideski

ISBN: 979-8-9880856-0-7

First paperback edition November 2023.

Edited by Jeni Chappelle

Cover art by Justin Snodgrass

For my fellow Truth Seekers.

Table of Contents

Foreword

By *Tomas Campbell, author of* My Big Toe
There is only one Big Truth, one correct understanding and explanation of the nature of our reality that includes both the objective and the subjective worlds of experience. However, there are many disparate paths that can lead you to this understanding of this Big Truth.

In *My Big Ego*, Vanessa shares her journey along the path she has created (and is still creating) through her choices. Not just a few big choices, but rather a long chain of everyday choices made over her life's accumulated experience that defines who and what Vanessa is at this moment.

We begin as potential with possibilities and every choice, small or large, redefines us by changing the array of our future possibilities and their associated probabilities. Thus, there are as many paths as people and all paths can take you to where you want to go. What sets Vanessa apart from most of us is that she eventually develops the courage to see bigger pictures (e.g., is her potential increasing or decreasing due to her choices), learn from the results of that assessment, and then act on the knowledge thus gained. This sounds like a very simple and straightforward thing to do, but very few people accomplish it in a major way. It is so much easier to blame the world in general, and other people in particular, for what isn't working in your life. The assumption of victimhood placates the fear that lives at the root of your being, and you immediately feel better.

Those who can see bigger pictures and learn from honest self-assessments generally make good teachers, because big picture self-awareness directly leads to other-awareness. People who are self-centered do not make good teachers… or good anything else. So, even though Vanessa's path is a very unusual one, try to find a way to apply her methodology of applying personal responsibility to life's problems to your problems and issues. Though her path is vastly different from yours, there are many lessons lurking inside her story that are both applicable and valuable to almost everyone.

Enjoy your read about this amazing woman pulling herself up by her bootstraps; going from being a self-absorbed abject failure to growing and thriving as a shining example of the ability of will and intention to create a reality of her choice. This is a personal metamorphosis that everyone can create, though few will.

Introduction

November 2015, I stumbled into the lecture hall at the Monroe Institute in Virginia. The Monroe Institute is known as a "modern-day Hogwarts for adults." It's the School of Magic where people from all over the world come to learn about different extrasensory perceptions such as telekinesis (moving objects with your mind), remote viewing (acquiring information about a distant person, place, or thing), astral projection, lucid dreaming, telepathy, and other paranormal abilities.

So there I was at the Monroe Institute, and Tom Campbell was at the front of the room, speaking to an intimate group of twenty-four people. After thirty-five years of wandering aimlessly around this planet trying to understand the purpose of it all, I'd finally settled into a classroom with Tom—physicist, consciousness researcher, and all-around awesome dude.

How did I even get here?

I remember being ten years old, looking around my bedroom, wondering, *What is all this?* In a state of bewilderment, I remember asking myself, *Why are we here? What's the point of this place?*

That initial spark of curiosity only grew stronger as I grew older. It inspired me to search for meaning and purpose, and for the past twenty-five years, this has been my mission; this search for a universal truth, purpose, and meaning has been the catalyst to numerous adventures, many interesting paths, and a multitude of different belief systems, philosophies, and walks of life.

Being raised by an atheist father and a non-religious mother helped me develop an open mind. By fourteen, I was largely responsible for forming my own beliefs. My parents divorced, and I lived with my mom, who gave me a lot of space to think for myself. This independence of thought gave me an insatiable curiosity to understand the nature of reality and my place within the universe. My immature mind couldn't comprehend life, meaning, and existence, which led me to experiment with drugs and alcohol. Eventually, my mom couldn't handle my wild ways, and she called social services in hopes that they might have a solution.

I found myself stumbling through existence, in and out of foster homes before finally settling in to live with my boyfriend at sixteen. This was when I came across the wisdom of Wayne Dyer and the first time I was introduced to ideas that really resonated with me. I found myself connecting with ideas like creating your own reality and manifesting your own destiny.

But by the time I discovered Wayne's material, I was already well entrenched in drugs and alcohol, and this took me away from fully getting a grip on reality. I was the poster child for someone who was lost and wandered down dark paths.

When I turned nineteen, the legal drinking age in Canada, I started waitressing at nightclubs and bars. I eventually fell for a bad boy. Within weeks of dating, he'd moved into my small apartment. A month later, we packed our bags and moved to Samoa. Our relationship quickly turned abusive, and this led to more drinking and more drugs.

The tipping point was our crystal meth addiction. Crystal meth is an evil substance—its only purpose is to destroy lives. It turned my life upside-down on three separate occasions. The third time was the charm that motivated me to move to the beach and sober up with some fresh air, salt water, and a whole lot of sunshine.

This all happened in my early twenties. After sobering up, I moved back to Vancouver, British Columbia, and lived a somewhat normal life. I got a job, bought a home, and thought, *Now what? Move up the corporate ladder?* No, thanks.

I quickly became bored of normal life and decided to continue my journey in search of truth. Only this time, I was a bit older and a tad wiser, so I opted out of drugs and alcohol and instead looked into religion, studied philosophy, and traveled. I moved to Asia to live in a Buddhist monastery, went to Europe for a pilgrimage, traveled to Panama, did a forty-day water fast… I was a girl on a mission! A mission to find truth. But through all my searching, I still felt lost.

After a few years of this, I threw up my hands and said, "The meaning of life? There is no meaning in life."

This was my new philosophy. Life is what you make of it.

So, I worked hard, got married, had kids, started a business, and did all the worldly things most of us in North America choose to do. I eventually got caught up in the rat race, and I replaced the pursuit of truth for the pursuit of money.

At thirty-five, I experienced a few milestone events. I said goodbye to a close friend, started over in business, and divorced my husband of seven years. This interruption in my life as I knew it gave me an opportunity to take a step back from the hustle and bustle my life had become and return to my search for meaning and purpose. I started reading many relevant books. I created a community for truth seekers, and within a few weeks of beginning this new chapter in my life, I came across Tom Campbell's teachings.

So, there I was at the Monroe Institute.

I got to spend the next six days learning from a NASA physicist who not only created a unified theory of everything, but also had over forty years of experience studying altered states of consciousness. I felt like a little girl in a candy shop. I was bursting with questions and eager to learn everything I could about life, purpose, and the nature of reality.

Many of us don't attempt to understand the nature of reality because it seems like a daunting task. It can feel like a major undertaking. Heck, Einstein spent the last two decades of his lifetime trying to understand it and failed.

But what if it's not as hard as we think it is? What if it were *easy* to understand? What if understanding the nature of reality was made simple?

That's what this book is—Understanding the Nature of Reality for Dummies.

My Big Ego is based on my personal experience learning about My Big Toe. In physics, a TOE is a "Theory of Everything." Tom Campbell calls his TOE "My Big Toe" because it's not a regular TOE that describes only this physical universe. It's a "big TOE" that explains our universe *and* phenomena found outside of the universe. This theory uncovers how the paranormal is actually just normal when understood from a big-picture perspective.

When I first came across Tom Campbell and MBT (My Big Toe), I was enthusiastically convinced that all the answers to the questions I'd been asking forever were found in his 822-page trilogy.

But as Tom would say, "This is *my* big theory of everything. You have to find your own."

Tom's work is simply a model to build upon. It serves as a template that helps to gain clarity and understanding. It's important to understand that this is only a model, a model that may help you gain a new perspective of consciousness, the universe, and our place within the big picture.

MBT comes from decades of Tom's research as an applied physicist and consciousness researcher. Unlike other physicists, Tom has developed the ability to explore altered states of consciousness and gather information from outside of this reality. The TOE Tom has derived is based on his interpretation of the information he received through decades of dedicated research. This book is my interpretation of MBT.

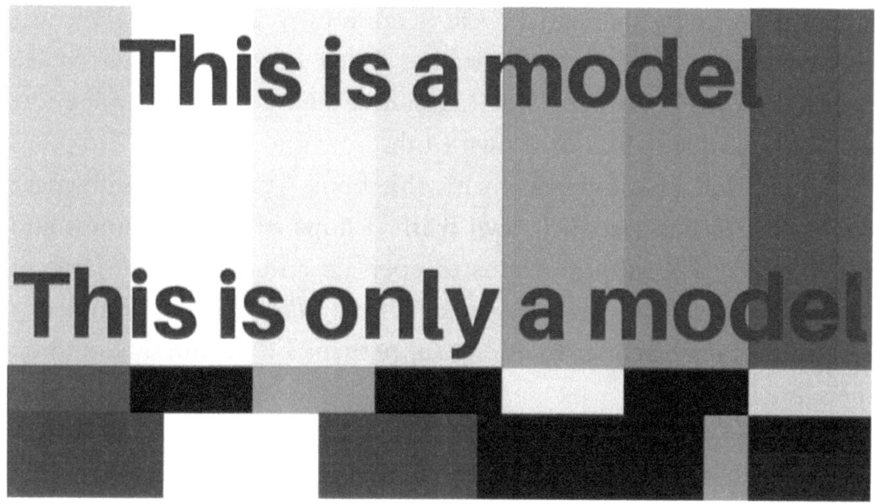

I encourage you to read this book with an open mind, but remain skeptical and check in with yourself to see if any of these words ring true. Trust yourself and listen to your own intuition.

As Tom would say, "Don't believe a word I say."

This is my experience, and perhaps you'll relate to some of the insights, but don't take on any of the ideas in this book as truth. The experiences I share are simply my interpretation of the truth I see.

During my first week at the Monroe Institute, I expressed to Tom that I wanted to thoroughly understand MBT and share it with others. Tom is a kind and encouraging man who supported my interest, and since then, I've been sharing MBT with my community. Together with a group of friends, we've expanded our community of truth seekers, which first started with the Conscious Connections group in 2015, to include new groups called Purpose, Clarity, and Love—A Practical Application of MBT. These groups meet once a week to explore the MBT model. We also have an MBT book club that meets online once a week to share insights, discuss ideas, and learn from each other. In addition to the above, we've created an MBT experiential group that explores metaphysics, meditation, and consciousness. Our intention is to help integrate this material from the intellectual level (the book club) into the being level (application and experiential). Our community of truth seekers has evolved into a non-profit organization called Low Entropy. We make personal growth and truth exploration accessible to all by creating safe spaces for people to find their own truth.

I have the same intention with this book—to create a safe space for readers to discover their own truth. I hope that my openness and vulnerability will support others to open up and look at the parts of themselves that have been neglected. In *My Big Ego*, I'm completely real, raw, and authentic. By doing so, perhaps I'll inspire others to do the same.

Life is so much easier when we don't have to be anyone other than who we truly are. I'm an average, everyday, regular woman who's working through her insecurities and doing the best she can to be a good momma, walk with integrity, and live a happy life. I'm far from being highly evolved, enlightened, or advanced. I won't try to inspire you by showing you how perfect I am. Instead, I hope to inspire you by showing you how I deal with my imperfections.

Spoiler alert: I can be clumsy at times, tripping over my ego, falling in my fear, and getting lost in self-doubt. I like to think that I'm able to pick up the pieces and start again, hopefully wiser than before, but I'll let you be the judge of that.

If there's one message I wish to convey to the world, it's this: *When you dare to explore the nature of reality, your experience of reality dramatically changes.*

Chapter 1: Learning the Rules Makes Playing the Game Easier

My Big Toe is a comprehensive model that describes… well, everything. It explains in detail how our universe came to be and the purpose of our existence as well as who and what we are. I'll give you a brief summary of the model, and I hope it will help you gain some insight into the meaning of life and our purpose here. If you need a more thorough explanation and require the technical and scientific aspects, I encourage you to explore Tom Campbell's teachings online and in written format. His material is widely available in print and online, and his trilogy can be found online for free through Google Books. If you prefer a synopsis of Tom's 822-page trilogy, then you've come to the right place.

Here's my interpretation of MBT summed up in a short story.

There once was an information system. Its name was Consciousness.

Like any information system, the purpose of Consciousness was to evolve, and it did this through lowering its entropy. Entropy is simply a physics term used to describe the measurement of disorder. The lower the disorder, the more a system evolves.

One day, Consciousness thought, *I wonder what it would be like if I partitioned off pieces of myself? What if I divided myself up into little subsets so I could experience myself outside this state of absolute, unbounded oneness?*

Immediately, the information system divided itself into pieces. As these pieces of consciousness interacted with each other, a lot of opportunities opened up. Consciousness realized it would be more helpful if there were structures in place, so it created various new realities. One reality in particular was created as an entropy-reducing playground. This reality was called the Universe. It was designed as a simulation, a sort of virtual reality for Consciousness to express itself through. The simulation included a ruleset with basic laws of nature, physics, biology, and chemistry. This ruleset helped to sustain the virtual reality long enough for Consciousness to adequately grow and evolve.

The simulation also included avatars for Consciousness to play through. The avatars ranged from low-sentient characters named fish and mammals to high-sentient characters called humans. Each avatar had free will which allowed the characters to make decisions that would either lower or raise the entropy of the information system.

When the Consciousness played a human character and made a decision with the intent of being more helpful, organized, and cooperative, naturally, the entropy reduced. On the other hand, when decisions were made with the intent of causing more harm, chaos, and destruction, the entropy increased.

The stage was set, and the experiment was underway.

The information system assumed it would instinctively make low-entropy decisions because the results in the simulation would be quite joyful and happy. However, this wasn't the case. It seemed the individuated pieces of Consciousness would often make high-entropy decisions regardless of how much sadness and sorrow they resulted in.

After a couple hundred thousand years of playing this simulation game called life in a reality frame of the Universe, Consciousness decided to drop hints for the players because they were taking the game too seriously. The information system gently reminded the players to chill out. The message of Consciousness was simple: Relax, peeps. This is just kindergarten for entropy reduction. Stop fighting on the playground!

If times get tough and you catch yourself taking life too seriously, it's probably because you're making high-entropy decisions. We all do this from time to time. The best thing to do is be gentle with yourself and practice patience. If you are consistent and determined to evolve, you'll see changes showing up as more love, peace, and harmony in your life, and this will inspire you to continue making low-entropy decisions.

The meaning of life is really quite simple. We're just here to grow up, and we do this through the decisions we make. When we make choices from a place of love and compassion, we progress and evolve toward an increased level of consciousness. When we make choices from fear and ego, we regress. Our evolution is dependent on our choices. Choose wisely.

I created a fun, five-minute animated video that illustrates the story above, and I showed it to some of my friends.

"Cool," they said. "Is that it?"

"Uh, yeah. Pretty much," I replied. "What more do you want?"

They often hesitate and say, "Well, it can't be that simple. There must be more to it."

This book is the answer to my friends' response. This is the more you've been asking for.

My Big Toe explains that there are two fundamental aspects to the nature of reality, and based on these two fundamentals, everything else can be derived. These two fundamentals are:

1. Consciousness exists and
2. Evolution exists.

So, what is consciousness? Most of us understand consciousness to be synonymous with awareness. However, it can be challenging to grasp this intangible concept and work with it. It helps if we understand the concept of consciousness as information. Consciousness is information or data.

For an information system to evolve, it needs to continue making new information. It does this through patterns and organization. Physicists describe this process as lowering entropy. To lower the entropy of an information system is to evolve the system and create new information by becoming more orderly, organized, and complex. When an information system evolves, it becomes more efficient by making new information that helps it grow and advance to new states.

Our starting point is consciousness. This is one of the fundamental building blocks. The second fundamental aspect is evolution. Consciousness and evolution both exist in harmony, and that's why the system works. For consciousness to survive, it must evolve, and it does this by lowering its entropy and growing into new states of being.

If we are consciousness at our core and our purpose is to grow and evolve by making low-entropy choices, then what does this look like on a practical level?

That is what this book is about. It will show you the practical aspects of My Big Toe. I'll give you many examples from my personal life that demonstrate what it looks like to apply the theory.

All the examples I share are uncensored and one hundred percent real. Most of the scenarios are baffling, and it can seem like I take three steps backward before finally taking one step forward. Sometimes, I like to make the same mistake a few times just to make sure I really get it the final time around. Now that I have a guidebook or an instruction manual for life, you'd think that I would learn a lot faster. However, that's not the case. I still make a lot of mistakes just for the fun of it.

I must admit, though, now that I understand the rules of the game, life has a new depth of significance. I haven't necessarily advanced my evolutionary growth, and I still get stuck at times, but I don't take things as seriously as I used to. I tend to treat life more like an experiment rather than a chore I've been cursed with. This attitude allows me to have fun.

So what exactly is this so-called game of life? What is this reality, and why are we here?

As stated in MBT, one of the ways consciousness has chosen to evolve itself is by interacting through various reality frames so it can experience itself outside its state of oneness. Each reality frame provides us with opportunities to make choices through the characters we play. All the beings (people, animals, critters) in our universe are opportunities for consciousness to express and experience itself. We experience this reality frame (the universe) as a strategy to further the evolution of our consciousness.

The reality frame that appears as the universe with all its different galaxies, solar systems, and planets, is simply a virtual reality for consciousness to lower its entropy and become more organized. We play in this virtual reality with eight billion human players who appear to be different from one another, and we are each given free will. Our ability to make choices with our free will is an integral part of lowering entropy to grow and evolve our consciousness. Without free will, we can't make choices, and we need to make choices to learn, grow, and evolve.

According to MBT, we are conscious beings, and we're all connected through consciousness. Certain functions are assigned to consciousness, and these designated responsibilities help consciousness evolve itself. The larger consciousness system (LCS) organizes and manages other aspects within consciousness. Within the LCS is The Big Computer (TBC). This is the function that computes reality for the players. The players are individuated units of consciousness (IUOC), and within these players is the free will awareness unit (FWAU). The function of the FWAU is to make choices for the avatar because this is how we evolve.

Here's a diagram to illustrate the information above.

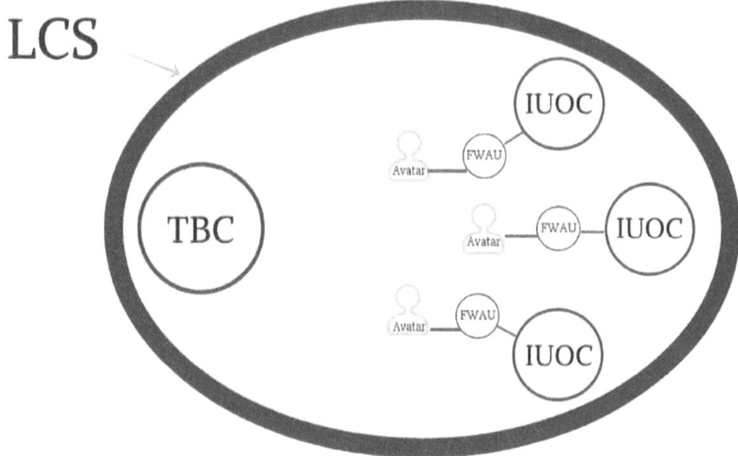

The last time I was at the Monroe Institute, I drew a similar diagram and showed it to Tom.

"Yes," he said. "It works like this, but stick with the big picture. Don't get lost in the details."

It's easy to get caught up in the details, but it's more productive to stay focused on the big picture. The metaphors Tom uses simply describe functions within consciousness. This is one way to interpret reality to help us harmoniously navigate this world.

These metaphors are new because they don't have any baggage or connotations attached to them. But the ideas aren't new. A lot of people will say, "Oh, the IUOC is like the soul or the higher self." Sure, you can call it that. MBT refers to the IUOC as the accumulating function. It accumulates information from all your incarnations, and it contains the quality of consciousness that's been earned through each incarnation or lifetime. MBT insists that IUOCs reincarnate into new reality frames because this is how we evolve. We must come back and experience new incarnations where we can apply what we've learned from our previous experiences. It's similar to a video game; it would be unheard of to simply have one life in a video game. When you play a new game, you die over and over again until you finally figure out how to get to the next level. The same is true in this reality frame; we need to experience many lifetimes to grow and evolve.

The FWAU is the piece of the IUOC that's partitioned off and immersed into the reality frame where the avatar is interacting with billions of other avatars. These avatars are a part of the reality frame and are being "played" by our FWAUs.

Each decision we make will either help us improve the quality of our consciousness by lowering our entropy or decrease the quality of our consciousness and raise our entropy. Again, entropy is simply a term used to describe the measurement of disorder. When information is highly disorganized, it has high entropy. For example, when we can't process our thoughts and we feel stressed out, we are experiencing a high-entropy state. On the other hand, when something is organized, it has low entropy, and we feel at peace.

Low-entropy choices move us forward toward a more organized state. When we work together and help one another, our social system becomes more efficient, more cooperative, and more organized. We put ourselves on the path toward lowering our collective entropy. The opposite is also true; when we isolate ourselves and think it's every man for himself, we stop improving the system. Chaos ensues, wars break out, and we devolve.

It seems quite simple when it's laid out like this. To evolve, we need to be more helpful toward one another. We need to be cooperative and have compassion for each other because this helps us to create a more harmonious humanity. And as each individuated unit of consciousness evolves, it helps the totality of consciousness evolve because we're all connected. On the other hand, if we choose to be selfish and only do what's good for ourselves, disregarding how it affects others, then we devolve and are out of alignment with our purpose. This feels destructive, lonely, and stressful.

If our purpose is to evolve our consciousness and we do this by making positive choices that come from love and compassion with the intent of helping others, then why aren't we doing this? Why do so many of us feel stuck, lost, and incomplete? Why are so many of us struggling with relationships, finances, or health? We want peace and joy. It sounds good. Many of us consider ourselves good people—or at least not evil. We're not purposefully making evil choices. So why is entropy so rampant?

Because many of us don't see the big picture, we don't know our purpose. Instead of seeing ourselves connected to each other, we feel alone, isolated, and stuck in our ways. Many teachings, philosophies, and spiritual paths share a piece of the big picture. Nearly all these teachings understand that love is the answer, but they don't include a logical process to explain how they've come to this conclusion. Often, teachings draw this conclusion through faith, dogma, or belief. My Big Toe includes the whole picture, and it logically explains the ideas behind it.

Please excuse the redundancy, but it's important to remember that MBT is only a metaphor. This model was designed to help us *understand* the truth. It's not the truth in itself. It's a model that can help us understand the nature of reality, and it can assist us in creating new meaningful change in the world. To make a significant change, we must dare to explore the nature of our own reality. It is my hope that, by changing the way we understand the nature of reality, our experience of reality will drastically shift.

Chapter 2: MBT in a Nutshell

MBT IS BASICALLY A FRAMEWORK to understand the nature of reality. It's another way to view our world and a different way to experience life. To really grasp this new understanding, it helps to suspend your current beliefs. But first, you have to take a look at what those beliefs are. How do we currently view the world, and what is our present reality?

For most of us, we look around and see a physical world with many different people, all separate from one another, cohabitating this planet we call Earth. Many of us walk through life not really knowing why we're here but doing our best to survive and make the most of our existence—an existence that pretty much seems unexplainable.

Have you ever pondered any of the following questions: Where did we come from? How did we get here? What are we doing here? Who am I, and what is the purpose of my life?

Humanity has tried to make sense of it all. Religion, philosophy, and science have dug deep into these questions. We're a fact-based society, and we decided that science had the facts. Our scientists became our truth-makers. They told us what to believe, and they distinguish what is true from what is false.

And what has science taught us? Do you remember the basic scientific principles you learned in school? Chemistry, biology, and physics. We learned about our physical world and how things work in this physical reality. Science taught us that matter is all there is. We learned that this physical reality is all that exists; nothing more, nothing less.

Do you know the definition of materialism? It's the belief that nothing exists except for matter. This is exactly what science taught us.

Materialism is ubiquitous. It's everywhere; it's what governs our life. It's our underlying belief system through which we view the world. We don't even realize this is a belief system because we believe it to be true. We consider our beliefs to be facts, and therefore, we don't question them. But what if there was another way to understand the nature of reality—a framework other than materialism?

Materialism causes us to feel alone in the universe. It causes us to feel separate from one another, and feeling separate is what causes us to compete with each other. Our outlook on the world today is based on survival of the fittest: *To get ahead, I need to look out for myself. I need to protect myself and put myself first and foremost.* This perspective has created a self-centered mentality, and this selfishness is at the root of much of our unhappiness.

When people only think about themselves, when it becomes all about us and getting our own needs met, we turn into a self-centered society. Materialism makes us focus on matter and material things. It teaches us that we need to get as much stuff as possible and protect all our stuff from others who might try and take it. Many are familiar with the saying, "He who dies with the most toys wins."

It sounds absurd. We know this doesn't make us happy. Sharing, caring, loving, and connecting—these are sources of happiness. Sharing our resources with one another and graciously giving. Caring enough to help each other through difficult times. Loving one another, recognizing our similarities, and respecting our differences. Connecting with people, spending quality time together.

But materialism doesn't support that. Instead, it leads people to see themselves as an island, to feel alone and to think, *What about me? What's in it for me?* This leads to greed, control, and power struggles. Taking advantage of people is common, accepted, and even revered. We see it in our movies, and we read about it in our books—us against them and me against the world. Materialism causes *stuff* to become more important than *relationships*.

But if not materialism, then what?

Eastern teachings from Buddhism, Hinduism, and Taoism all share a common theme that approaches reality from a different perspective. If you aren't interested in religion, let's bring it back to the West and look at the teachings of Plato, Socrates, and Aristotle. These great minds and esoteric teachings show us that there is an alternative to materialism. Each thinker shared a common theme. They all viewed our reality as an illusion, a dream—shadows on the wall. Rather than this being a material-based reality, what if we understood this reality to be information based?

Physicists knew that materialism was incorrect nearly one hundred years ago, but they couldn't explain it back then. I'm referencing extraordinary thinkers such as Schrodinger, Bohr, and Einstein. These intellectuals and geniuses knew materialism was incorrect, but back then, they had no other reference to view reality through, so they couldn't make sense of it. Scientists needed to believe in materialism until we had a bigger picture.

The era we live in today has that bigger picture. We live in the information age; we can now comprehend our reality through a different framework. We no longer need materialism to understand our existence.

What does that even mean? What is an information-based reality?

For centuries, scientists have believed that reality is made of particles.[1] But one hundred years ago, physicists discovered that, when matter is examined from a subatomic level, we find that atoms are 99.99% empty space. We also discovered action at a distance, the concept that an object can be affected without being physically touched by another object. Scientists were baffled. They couldn't make sense of this. Einstein referred to much of this phenomenon as "spooky."[2]

---

[1] Feynman, Richard. "Nanotechnology: There's Plenty of Room at the Bottom." *Engineering and Science (Caltech Magazine)* Feb. 1960.

[2] Muller, Andreas. "What Is Quantum Entanglement? A Physicist Explains Einstein's 'Spooky Action at a Distance." *Astronomy,* 7 Oct. 2022, astronomy.com/ news/2022/10/what-is-quantum-entanglement. Accessed 23 Mar. 2023.

Fast-forward to today, where we live in the information age and physicists have a better reference to understand our reality. We're beginning to see that our reality is just data. Nothing is made of matter; it's all just information. We live in what appears to be a virtual reality.

Remember to do your best to suspend your beliefs and be curious. As Wayne Dyer said, "The highest form of ignorance is when you reject something you don't know anything about." Consider the possibility and ask yourself, *What if there's some truth to this?*

For the most part, we form beliefs to feel safe because the unknown can be scary. When we don't know what something is or what something means, it creates a lot of uncertainty, and that can feel uncomfortable. Rather than staying in this uncomfortable feeling, we make up a belief and tell ourselves we know what it means.

Although our beliefs give us a sense of certainty, safety, and security, they also cut us off from discovering other possibilities. When we believe one thing to be true, we close our mind to new ideas. We stop seeing different perspectives, and we can't see new opportunities.

I invite you to suspend your beliefs, if only temporarily. After this is over, you can go back to your old beliefs if you so choose. For now, I encourage you to open your mind, expand your vision, and consider new possibilities. Do your best to embrace the unknown, and as Tom would say, "Live gracefully with uncertainty."

Once we understand this reality is information-based and what we're experiencing here is virtual, we'll come to understand that consciousness created this virtual reality. Consciousness is what's real; consciousness is fundamental. We are all a part of this consciousness. Not us, our physical bodies—because, remember, our physical bodies are part of this virtual reality frame. Beyond this illusory existence, our consciousness is the cause of this reality frame.

This understanding will lead us to the question of why. Why did we, as consciousness, create this reality? We created this reality as a strategy that we, as consciousness, use to evolve. How do things evolve? Basically, evolution is the process of improvement. Something grows and improves over time. It evolves by getting better and becoming more efficient. Consciousness does this as well. It needs to evolve.

This reality—the universe—that we're experiencing is a strategy for us to further our growth and evolve. Parts of the whole, pieces of consciousness, are expressed through you and me. Every single one of us have parts to play. We each contribute to the evolutionary progress of the whole. When I say every single one of us, I'm referring to our real essence, our fundamental nature as consciousness.

It's our consciousness that's real. Our consciousness is playing this game called life in a virtual reality called the universe. Our ruleset, i.e., our chemistry and physics, manage the stage we play on and interact with, while another part of our ruleset, our biology, supports the growth and evolution of the avatars, the characters that we get to play in this game of life.

So how do we contribute to the evolutionary progress of the whole? How do we help the totality of us all as consciousness to evolve? We do this by making choices that lead to efficiency. We evolve by cooperating and working together. When we cooperate and work together, things become more efficient. Everything improves. Life, existence, and our world gets better. By logical deduction, we can conclude that cooperation and caring are essential. Compared to materialism, this seems like a far better solution to me!

Compassion and love are better understood when we realize this reality is virtual. It's an information-based reality. This concept isn't new. Over 2,500 years ago, Siddhartha Gautama, the Buddha, expressed that life is an illusion. Buddhism, Taoism, Hinduism, Western philosophy, Eastern tradition—they've all known this to be true, but it's stayed in the margins because science couldn't prove it.

Scientists couldn't make sense of it—that is, until now. Now, physicists are beginning to puzzle through it. They're starting to understand what Einstein alluded to when he said, "Reality is merely an illusion, albeit a very persistent one."

They're beginning to understand that our reality is virtual.

This new understanding puts us on the brink of a major paradigm shift, moving us away from the materialism that results in fear, ego, and greed, and moving us toward an information-based reality that results in love, peace, and compassion.

This gives us a framework to understand why we're here. We begin to see that we're not here to get as much stuff as possible and compete with each other for resources. We're not here to be self-centered and only think about ourselves. We're actually here to help one another, to cooperate, and to work together. We're here to connect with each other, to create peaceful communities, loving relationships, and joyous experiences.

To make this shift, it is helpful to start by understanding that this "physical world" isn't made of matter.

It's virtual.

This moves us away from materialism, and we can take the emphasis away from physical matter. We can stop making material things so important and instead shift our attention toward consciousness. When we do this, we start making relationships more important. We start cultivating new values, and we focus on helping, supporting, and encouraging one another.

This understanding will help us see that life is the lesson and love is the answer.

Chapter 3: MBT as a Model of Reality

LOVE IS THE RESULT OF a low-entropy state, and the opposite is also true. Fear is the result of a high-entropy state. To lower our entropy, we must let go of our fear.

The number one cause for our struggles is fear. Fear is what prevents us from evolving. Fear is what stops us from following our purpose. Fear is what we need to let go of to move forward on our evolutionary journey toward an improved quality of consciousness. This book is a practical guide with the intent of helping you identify your subtle fears and align with your purpose to improve your being, grow into love, lower your entropy, and evolve your own quality of consciousness. We'll do this by visiting some real-life examples that will allow you to relate this model back to your own life.

But before we get started on the practical application, let's visit fear more closely and explore what fear is, where it comes from, why it's important to let go of fear, and how this will help us evolve.

Many of us have heard the acronym for fear as "false evidence appearing real," or the more playful approach, "f-ck everything and run." Both are true to a certain extent, but let's take a look at the first example. Fear is "false evidence appearing real." This implies that fear doesn't exist; the mind only makes it so.

For example, let's say you're a two-year-old child and you're playing with a stray dog who happens to bite your leg. As a child, you're scared. You're in pain, and you're afraid the dog will bite you again. But then your mother brings you to safety, and you're no longer afraid.

A year later, you're playing at the park, and a dog comes up to you and sniffs you. You immediately freak out and start crying, fearing the dog will bite you again, just like the last dog. However, this is a friendly dog. He just wants to sniff you. There's no need to be fearful. It's simply your mind linking the event to a trauma that occurred a year ago.

In this example, the fear is simply false evidence appearing real because there really is no need to feel afraid. However, the emotion is real for you. You're experiencing this fear for a reason, and it's up to you to understand the fear, then decide to let it go. On the other hand, if you choose to keep this fear, you'll live the rest of your life afraid of dogs, all because of an event that happened when you were two years old. This is a basic example that shows how most of our fears are simply false evidence appearing real. There's no need to be afraid.

But why do we feel fear in the first place? Isn't it designed to keep us safe? Why would we want to get rid of fear when it protects us?

Fear is an emotion; it's part of who we are. Yes, in the past, it helped to keep us safe. In primitive times, it was a helpful tool that gave us the flight-or-fight response. But as the human race continues to evolve as a species, fear no longer serves us.

I often hear the argument, "But if I see a vicious dog foaming at the mouth, growling and ready to attack, it's my fear that prompts me to escape and run away from the dangerous animal."

A lot of us think it's fear that protects us, but it's actually our intelligence that keeps us safe. If this situation occurs, your fear will cause you to panic and run away, in which case, the dog may chase you and take you down. Or perhaps your fear will cause you to fight and attack the dog before it hurts you. Either option puts you and the dog in an unfavorable situation. Without the fear causing your fight or flight, you could operate from a more grounded, centered, and calm place. You could think clearly. You could see a bigger picture, and more decisions would become available. You may notice the dog is chained up and he's growling at a cat behind you. Or perhaps the dog softens up when he notices your calm demeanor. Letting go of fear opens you up to many different possibilities absent in the face of fear.

When we're in a fearful state, it causes us to act in irrational ways. It's much more efficient for us to operate from a calm place and use our intelligence.

But how does one determine their own fears?

Many masculine personalities will assert that they're fearless and nothing scares them. Fear doesn't always appear as a frightened response. Fear manifests itself in many different forms. To identify one's fears, it helps to pay attention to negative emotions. All negative emotions stem from fear. If you're feeling angry, irritated, or upset, honestly ask yourself why you're feeling that way. This will help you trace the negative emotion back to the original fear.

For example, if you're in a hurry and you're waiting in line at the store, stuck behind a super slow customer, and you find yourself frustrated, there's a fear behind that frustration. It could be a fear of being late for an event where people may judge you for your tardiness or the fear of missing an important meeting. There are many possible fears, and most of them trace back to the fear of not being able to handle the consequences or the fear of being inadequate.

Once you start identifying your fears, you may be overwhelmed by the amount of fear you do have. If this happens, do your best not to judge, shame, or blame yourself. If anything, you can choose to be happy about your decision to face your fears once and for all.

Most of us sweep our fears under the rug, and we don't admit to ourselves or to others that our fear exists. When this happens, we deny an aspect of ourselves, and we become fragmented individuals who walk around with feelings of uncertainty. Many of us feel lost and incomplete, and with good reason. When we avoid our fear, we've lost a part of ourselves. Pretending our insecurities don't exist is denying an aspect of who we truly are.

Sigmund Freud is known as the Father of Psychology. Freud taught us about the unconscious mind, which he broke into a topographical map of id, ego, and superego. The id is our instinctive impulses, the ego represents a person's sense of identity, and the superego is one's consciousness or the moral compass that mitigates between the id and the ego. Much of today's applied psychology is based on the premise that our unconscious mind is relevant to our experience. The unconscious and the subconscious are often used interchangeably.

The subconscious and the ego are now part of our common language, and most people would agree we all have these mental facilities.

For most of my life, I've been extremely interested in the psyche. I've always been curious as to why people behave the way they do because I find people fascinating. We all have such unique experiences that shape us, and I'm interested in learning about the many ways we show up. How do we humans work, why do we do the things we do, and what makes us behave in self-destructive ways? I've been specifically keen in learning about the human condition, how we can change our behavior, and why change feels so difficult.

Most of the research I've found points back to the unconscious mind. To create sustainable, permanent change, we must work with the unconscious mind. This is why we've developed a plethora of methods to attempt to change our unconscious habits. These methods range from hypnosis to NLP (neuro linguistic programming), EFT (emotional freedom technique), PSYCH-K (a method of transforming limiting beliefs into supportive beliefs at the subconscious level)… the list goes on. We have many strategies to help us make the unconscious conscious and thereby more accessible so we can make conscious choices to change what we're doing.

I've spent the last two decades attempting to uncover the hidden parts of myself that psychology claims are buried deep within the depths of my unconscious mind. I've been curious to know what's in there. If parts of who I am are hidden deep within, I want to find these aspects of myself. I must discover what's lurking in the shadows of my psyche. I want to expose the monsters of my past and dance with my inner demons.

However, there are innumerable philosophies about the psyche and a variety of physiological schools with different techniques. So, who's right? What's the best route to truly know yourself? It seems there are as many routes of inquiry as there are types of religion. With everyone preaching their field is the best, that their ideologies are superior, how can we know who or what route to trust? What is the *truth?*

Many of us have aspects of the truth, but I have yet to discover the whole truth. Perhaps this is a journey that never ends. The truth continues to evolve, and we continue to seek it. When referring to his MBT model, Tom Campbell explains, "There is but one truth. However, there are many expressions of it." The Bible states in John 8:32, "The truth shall set you free." And yet, in the movie, *A Few Good Men*, we're told that we "can't handle the truth."

Okay, I'm not sure how credible that last quote is. But the words are quite powerful.

According to MBT, we can't handle the truth of who we are. Therefore, we disown parts of ourselves and relegate the parts of ourselves we don't like to the unconscious mind. The parts of ourselves we don't like—those are our fears.

Why do we sweep our fear under the rug?

For many of us, it's too uncomfortable to face our fear. In turn, we end up living more unconsciously than we have to. Rather than braving what makes us uncomfortable, we take the easy path. We suppress the fears that haunt us, and we label this our subconscious mind. To keep these fears suppressed, we turn to mind-numbing activities to avoid how we really feel. It may seem a lot easier to avoid our feelings by checking out in front of the TV, eating unhealthy processed food, buying things we can't afford, drinking alcohol to make us even more dissociated… Pick your vice of choice. As a result, we have a culture cashing in on our addictions to avoidance—to television, sugar, alcohol, adrenaline, shopping, sex, drugs, etc. It's evident that we've become a society where it's socially acceptable to ignore our fears and insecurities to pretend we have it all together.

But there's a shift occurring. A movement has started, arising from enough of us being done with sleepwalking our way through life. Enough of us have come to a point where we know it's time to wake up and do what we came to this world to do. As a result, we see meditation becoming more mainstream, consciousness centers opening up, and an increased interest in neuroscience and personal development.

How do we become a part of this change? How do we actualize our full potential and align with our purpose to improve the quality of our consciousness? How do we evolve and ultimately grow up? Grow up in an evolutionary sense; grow and improve the quality of our consciousness. The first step sounds simple, but it's the most important step you can take.

You must *want* to grow up.

Chapter 4: Growing Up

Having the intent to improve your quality of consciousness and evolve your being is the most important decision you can make. Set this as your intention, and everything else will fall into place. The key to this is that your intention must come from the being level. What I mean by this is you must really want to *grow up* and evolve. You must have a strong, steady intent to let go of your fear and become a more loving and compassionate being. If this all sounds like a great idea and you think it might create some value in your life, if you think you might give this a try, then it's not coming from the being level. It's simply coming from your intellect.

The being level is who you really are at your core, whereas the intellect is often obscured by fear and taken over by the ego. To live at the being level, it's mandatory to get in touch with your emotions because your emotions come from the being level. Your emotions are the real, unadulterated, unapologetic, you. Emotions come from our authentic self. Our emotions are the truth of who we really are. We don't control our emotions; they just happen. Most of us have bottled up our emotions and are so out of touch with how we feel that we don't even know who we truly are.

How do we get in touch with our emotions? We need to learn how to feel our way through life. This can be a major shift in the way we do things because we've been conditioned to act from intellect.

It's helpful to see emotions as a feedback indicator. Our emotions can point out areas where we need to pay attention on our journey of spiritual development and our path toward lowering entropy. Negative emotions show us where we're still holding on to fear. They point us in the direction of where we still have work to do.

The majority of us have been raised in a culture that teaches us to hide our emotions. Many of us have been taught that showing our emotions is a sign of weakness. Therefore, we've developed an idea of who we think we should be, and this is the image we show to the world. Some people refer to this image as our ego. We create this image as a means to keep us safe. We're taught that, if we let others see our real emotions, we could get hurt, so we put up a façade of the type of person we think others will approve of. If we're getting approval from others, if others like us, then they won't hurt us. We think this façade will protect us.

Instead of trusting ourselves and getting in touch with our emotions, we've abandoned ourselves and shut out our emotions to deal with the outside world. Many of us walk around as fragmented individuals. In fact, Freud's model depicts the human psyche as a segregated entity. We're described as having a subconscious mind that drives most of our actions and behaviors, without being aware of the thoughts and feelings in that subconscious mind. This is why so many of us have a hard time changing our habits and behaviors: the alcoholic can't seem to stop drinking when it's clearly destroying her life; the obese father who can't stop eating when it's creating numerous health problems; the procrastinator who can't stop procrastinating; etc.

We try to make changes from our conscious mind, but it seems that our subconscious mind is constantly sabotaging us. When we look at this closely, we see that it's our fear preventing us from moving in the direction our conscious mind wants to go.

For example, weight loss is a multibillion-dollar industry because many of us have fear that sabotages our effort to lose weight. If we're fearful of being hurt, our fear says, *Yes, eat that extra helping. It will keep you overweight and protect you from bad people.* Our conscious mind has no idea what's going on because it avoids fear at all costs. We then become frustrated because we keep saying we want to lose weight and be healthy, but our behaviors and actions don't align with what our conscious mind tells us to do.

It's our fear of not being good enough that prevents us from going for that promotion. *We don't belong in the upper class. We need to stay in our comfort zone.* Meanwhile, our conscious mind can't figure out why we just can't seem to get ahead.

This is the human dilemma. We say we want something—a healthy body, a strong mind, more money, lots of knowledge, a supportive spouse, etc.—but we keep falling short. This dilemma is what fuels the self- help gurus and perpetuates sales of personal development courses and self-help books. We're always searching; we all want something. Some of us may simply want to find out what it is we truly want. Many of us are simply searching for purpose.

It's true that we're fragmented individuals, but we weren't designed to be this way. We've become fragmented because we've chosen to disown parts of ourselves. We've trained ourselves not to feel our emotions and sweep our negative feelings under the rug. Many of us on this planet feel disconnected. We feel like something's missing in our lives. But the thing that's missing is *you*. We've misplaced ourselves; we've shut ourselves out by ignoring and dismissing our emotions.

To embark upon the journey of finding ourselves, to answer the age-old question *Who am I?*, we must learn to connect with our emotions and rediscover the innocence we shunned long ago. To know thyself is one of the most important things one can do. It's from this level of understanding that we can courageously face our fears.

Here is a process to help you begin to "know thyself."

First, you must be honest with yourself and start telling yourself the truth. So often, we lie to ourselves to feel good. We tell ourselves we're choosing to indulge in a big bowl of ice cream because we deserve it, we buy a pair of expensive shoes we can't afford because we're worth it, we cheat on our spouse because they take us for granted… Lies, lies, *lies!* If we really want to know ourselves, align with our purpose, and evolve into our fullest potential, then we need to start telling the truth.

Here's a common example: When you're blaming or criticizing another, it's usually because you don't want to face your own truth. It can seem easier to point out someone else's faults rather than admit something about yourself. If you catch yourself blaming others for the way you feel, turn it around and take responsibility for your own reaction. When you start being honest with yourself and you grow your courage to tell yourself the truth, no matter how uncomfortable it may feel, you begin the process of growing up.

The next step is acceptance. Many of us are in denial because the truth may be uncomfortable and even painful to endure. Rather than feel uncomfortable, we tell ourselves ignorance is bliss.

I remember being excited about *Cowspiracy*, a documentary on the secrets and sustainability of animal agriculture. I shared my excitement with my friends, but many responded with, "Well, I don't want to know about the animal agriculture industry. If I do, I'll have to change. If I don't know, then I can continue to enjoy my steak guilt-free." I was surprised by this response, but I understand how difficult change can be, so I empathize because I'm ignorant at times too.

What's the underlying cause for this attitude? Fear.

It always comes back to fear. In this case, it could be fear of the unknown. *Oh, no! What will happen if we know the truth about animal agriculture? I may never be able to enjoy a bacon cheeseburger again!* Any vegan or vegetarian would say, yes, you can have a healthy alternative that tastes way better, is better for the environment, costs you less, and doesn't involve harming another living being for your enjoyment.

But, out of fear, the carnivore may cling to his ignorance and remain in his comfort zone.

I'm by no means knocking meat-eaters. I've struggled to maintain a vegan lifestyle, and I'm currently back to eating meat myself. I know firsthand the lure of the meat industry. I'm simply giving this example to demonstrate how many of us convince ourselves that ignorance is bliss. However, once we let go of this belief, we will begin to see how the truth can set us free.

As we begin to tell ourselves the truth, we must accept new insights about who we are.

Please let that last line sink in. As we begin to tell ourselves the truth, we must accept our new insights about who we are. As we do this, we'll notice that sometimes we're happy with who we are. We're pleased with the choices that come from a place of love and compassion.

The opposite is also true. We won't be as excited about the decisions based on fear and a sense of selfishness. We'll most likely want to deny or justify this negative aspect of who we are. The latter can be the tricky part. We often won't recognize the ego trying to sneak in and justify our behaviors, but this takes us away from accepting who we really are. This is where a sense of humility, intuition, and big-picture thinking can help us learn to be honest with ourselves and learn to accept who we are at our core.

I'll share an example from my own life. I realize that this may seem hard to follow because it's going on behind the scenes from the unconscious mind. It is, in fact, the dialogue of my fear. But when we're in touch with our fear—when we acknowledge that dialogue—we pull the curtain back and expose the unconscious mind.

Here is my naked mind, fears and all. Please, don't judge it. We just started going to the gym. What I mean is I'm still a work in progress, and I have a long way to go.

I work for an organization that helps people transform their lives through a series of weekend workshops and other programs up to ninety days long. Their mission is to strengthen the fabric of the world through a commitment to lifelong learning and fostering meaningful connection in community. The company hired me based on the caveat that they would put me through all their programs so I could learn their culture, identify their philosophy, and discover their teachings.

Over the weekend, I took one of their three-day intensive workshops. This program creates a safe space for people to look closely at their self-limiting beliefs. In our workshop, we had twenty-five participants, one main facilitator, and five assistants. There was a mic at the front of the room, and throughout the program, participants were asked if they would like to share their thoughts with everyone. At one point, we were asked to share an area in our lives we would like to improve and what self-limiting belief was preventing us from moving forward in that area.

I volunteered to share. Since I like to apply the MBT model, I understand that our beliefs are a product of our fear, so I went straight to the fear and identified my fear of inadequacy.

I was overwhelmed by the amount of fear that came up for me. An immense amount of guilt arose as I explored my fear of inadequacy. I acknowledged the fear, allowed myself to fully feel it rather than suppress it, and accepted it as my own. My fear of inadequacy manifested itself as guilt. I felt guilty for not spending more quality time with my children, and as I shared this, I began to cry in front of everyone. In the past, every time these guilty feelings came up, I would simply ignore them or justify the feelings and tell myself that everything was fine.

This is what it would look like:

I would be driving, in a meeting, or doing something outside of my home, and I would think, *I need to spend more time with my kids.* My fear would be subtle. *It's so much work managing my patience with my kids,* I'd think, and my ego would try to cover up my fear by saying, *The kids are fine. They're with your mom, and you have other things that need your attention right now.*

Yes, I would agree with my sneaky little ego. *You're right. I have other things that need my attention right now, and my kids are fine with my mom.*

See how disconnected this is? When I type it out, it sounds dysfunctional and irrational. Rather than facing the fear directly, I chose to listen to the ego. The ego was the logic I used to justify my own behavior so I wouldn't have to acknowledge the fear because the fear was too uncomfortable to face. This is an example of how the ego tries to cover up the fear and justify the behavior instead dealing directly with the real root of the emotion.

The fear came up as, *It's hard work managing my patience with my kids.* In other words, I often get frustrated when I'm parenting, and this is because my fear of inadequacy gets triggered. Parenting exposes my fear of not being good enough.

When I'm honest with myself, I can see the truth: I'm being selfish because I'm being driven by my fear of inadequacy. I have a choice here. I can either a) choose to accept this new insight about myself; or b) let my ego justify my behavior and continue to deny my fear.

I've chosen option A. I accept this new insight about myself, and with this awareness, I'm determined to change. I've made a commitment to myself to be more present with my children and spend more quality time with them. By having a clear, focused intent, my behavior and actions reflect my decision.

My babies are my greatest teachers. They show me my impatience, my frustration, and my anger. My kids are the only beings with the ability to activate my fear to such a large degree, and for that, I'm incredibly grateful, though I don't always recognize it in moments when I'm overcome with frustration.

Sometimes, my kids don't listen to me. I ask them to put their toys away, brush their teeth, and get ready for school. I'm constantly reminding them, and sometimes, they choose not to hear me. Other times, my children whine. They might whine about having to go to sleep so early, or they might complain about eating their veggies, doing their homework, taking a bath, or anything else they don't feel like doing. These are things that trigger me, and on occasion, I've yelled at my kids for that reason. In fact, I've even felt rage come up while parenting them.

See how wonderful they are?

I don't yell at my friends. I don't feel rage when my students, colleagues, strangers, or other family members complain and don't listen to me. My wonderful children are closest to my heart, and they're the ones who help me uncover all my deep fears and insecurities.

Thank you, Noah and Nala.

When we start learning self-acceptance, we cultivate and strengthen a distinct awareness of our feelings and emotions. It's easy to notice the big emotions or reactions we experience such as happiness, joy, anger, or sadness. Being mindful of how we're feeling from moment to moment is what helps us grow.

This leads us to the third step—develop an awareness of your emotions on a consistent basis. Awareness will help you get in touch with how you feel, which is, in essence, who you are. Remember, your feelings and emotions come from the being level; this is who you are at the core. You may act a particular way, but how you feel is the real you.

When we increase our awareness of our feelings, we no longer lash out with big emotions like I did when I cried in front of everyone at the workshop. I've heard Tom Campbell state that, "emotions burst out of nowhere when we are not living out of the being level."

Clearly, I'm not living out of the being level, but I'm dedicated to doing the work that helps me get there, the work that helps me become more congruent with who I truly am at my core. I have a strong, steady intent to evolve the quality of my consciousness, to lower entropy and make choices that come from love. As long as we have a strong intent to grow up, we will. Some simply take longer than others, and I'm no exception to this rule.

The fourth and final step is to trust yourself. This helps you to align who you think you should be with who you really are. When you trust your feelings and emotions, you no longer have to pretend to feel differently. You can honor yourself by owning your feelings.

Here's the strategy that I explained above. This method may help you learn to understand your true self and make the unconscious conscious.

Steps to help you know thyself:

1. Tell the truth and be honest with yourself.
2. Accept yourself for where you are on your journey. Some days, you may feel elated about your progress. Other days, you may feel disappointed. Do your best to accept where you are and don't beat yourself up.
3. Develop a keen awareness of your emotions on a consistent basis.
4. Trust yourself.

These steps are as simple or as complicated as you make them. Remember, real change occurs on a deeper being level, not the intellectual level. These steps are simply tools to help you reach that deeper level of who you really are beyond your ego and beliefs.

Chapter 5: Why We Exist

"Manipulating things in this physical matter reality to suit your needs is all well and good, but understanding the big picture is vastly more significant."

—Tom Campbell

THIS IS THE BIG PICTURE:

WE ARE CONSCIOUSNESS, AND WE need to evolve. When we make decisions based on love, we evolve the quality of our consciousness. Love-based decisions lead to more harmony, efficiency, and cooperation. Everything works better when we come from love. Love is the answer.

That's it. It really is that simple. Sometimes, when things seem this simple, we don't recognize the substance. So let me elaborate more and give you your money's worth.

We've been conditioned by a worldview called materialism. This philosophy is the belief that matter is the only thing that exists. Materialism tells us that all things in the universe, including mankind, are necessarily restricted to operate within the bounds of physical laws.

Materialism is an outdated concept that has led us to the current state of the world we live in today, a world that's ruled by fear. Fear breeds ego, greed, selfishness, and destruction. A worldview based on materialism keeps us separate. It keeps us divided and apart, when what we really need is to come together and unite.

Materialism has also taught us that we're separate and everything outside of us is external. This philosophy has influenced the habitual blame game where the cause of our unhappiness is always outside of us. Materialism insists that we relegate responsibility away from ourselves and onto some other person, place, or thing.

This is why we need a paradigm shift to move us away from materialism and bring us toward a new understanding of the nature of reality. This is no small feat, but it's the direction we're headed in. It won't happen overnight, but it's definitely happening. So buckle up and enjoy the ride!

Humanity has experienced several major paradigm shifts. One of the most notable was the shift from the geocentric view that the sun revolves around the Earth to the heliocentric view, the idea that the Earth revolves around the sun. It took a couple centuries for this new understanding to become fully accepted by the masses, but let's hope it won't take as long for our current paradigm shift to occur.

The current fundamental paradigm shift is the shift from materialism to consciousness. This will be the largest, most positive paradigm shift humanity has ever experienced. This is an amazing time to be alive! We also need to keep in mind that we can shout the truth from the rooftops, but it will fall on deaf ears when we are overcome by fear, ego, and belief.

We can't force new information onto people. All we can do is evolve our own quality of consciousness. If we want to help others and show them a bigger picture, the best thing we can do is respect them and treat them with kindness and compassion. Remember, when we're loving and compassionate with others, it helps them come to a better place. The way for us to be helpful is to always make it a habit to respond with love.

This is one of my favorite quotes: "I did not come to teach you. I came to love you. Love will teach you." An ego-free philosophy by an unknown author.

Why is it important to understand the big picture? How does this help us?

We often get stuck. Stuck in our thoughts, beliefs, opinions, and our limited perspectives. We face a lot of challenges throughout our lifetimes, and it can be difficult to pull ourselves out of those challenges when we're stuck in the middle of them. We can find ourselves spinning our wheels, trying to force our way out, trying to control the situation and unconsciously manipulating things to be the way we want them to be.

For example, when my husband and I divorced, I met someone new, and my ex-husband was unhappy with me because I introduced my new partner to our children. My ex-husband resented me and told me our friendship was over.

I was upset because I wanted a happy co-parenting relationship with him. For weeks, I tried to mend our friendship, but I was unable to resolve anything or fix our relationship. I was trying to make him see my perspective. I wanted to force my ideas onto him because my ideas were obviously better than his own. My ego was in charge, and it was trying to control the situation. This wasn't working very well, and I finally accepted the situation as it was.

I chose to accept where he was coming from, and I let go of what I wanted. I chose to see a bigger picture. I realize now that whenever I try to control, manipulate, or force others to understand me, listen to me, or do what I want them to do, it's usually because I'm making it all about me. I'm stuck in my own little picture.

Alternatively, when I remember the big picture—when I remember my purpose here and I recall what my mission is—I can pull myself out of my limited perspective and open myself up to a bigger understanding.

Rather than trying to force a friendship on my ex-husband, I reminded myself that my purpose is to evolve into love and let go of fear. Forcing people to see things my way is not an act of love.

While I was stuck in my little picture, I didn't see that I was trying to force anything onto anyone. Instead, my ego did a great job of justifying my position and asserting I was right. It looked a little something like this: *I want us to have a friendship because our kids will benefit from seeing their parents cooperate and approach co-parenting from such a mature place of love. Our family will be much more functional and compassionate when my ex-husband and I are friends. He needs to understand this so we can help our children feel more confident and secure.*

These statements sound logical. They seem to be reasonable explanations as to why it's important to maintain a friendship with my ex-husband. But if I remove the limiting lens I view my reality through, if I remember the big picture and understand my purpose here, I remind myself that I'm here to evolve into love and focus on others. I'm not here to force my position onto others. I want to put others first and expand my perspective to include other people, not just myself.

Fear shrinks our vision. It limits our perspective, and love expands our sight. It deepens our understanding.

Intellectually, I understand this. But I hadn't integrated these ideas at the being level, and I was coming from fear and ego. My ego was trying to convince me I was making it about others, that I was thinking about the kids and what's best for them. I was trying to control and force the situation into what I knew was best for everybody. This is clearly ego at its finest.

The interesting thing is, the moment I stopped trying to control things and walked away from the idea of making us have a healthy friendship, a healthy relationship naturally formed. Today, we have a mature co-parenting relationship.

Our divorce has taught me some of my most valuable lessons in this lifetime. Letting go of the need to control has been an invaluable lesson that has created freedom, ease, and peace in my world.

It's fun to play in this world of form, to travel to exotic destinations, meet interesting people, have nice things, and experience exciting adventures. All of this is great, and it's part of our worldly experience. We get to play in this reality and have fun with all the props, characters, and scenes. It helps to remember the line from Shakespeare's play, *As You Like It*: "All the world's a stage, and all the men and women merely players."[3] Don't get attached to the players, props, and scenes. Enjoy them and celebrate life, but remember the big picture.

---

[3] William, Shakespeare. *As You Like It. Digireads.Com Publishing*, 2016.

Unlike a play, we're here to do more than entertain. We're here to learn, to grow, and, ultimately, to love. We often become enamored by the players, captivated by the scenes, and fascinated by the props. This is likely to happen when we lose sight of the big picture. If we don't know why we're here, it's easy to find distractions that keep us forever entertained in this world of form, and there's absolutely nothing wrong with this. Most of us will continue to incarnate into this reality for entertainment and pleasure, bearing in mind the contrast that comes with this.

When we live our life in the pursuit of pleasure, we're subject to life not meeting our expectations. This can leave us feeling upset and discouraged. At times, we may experience joy and happiness. Other times, we may experience disappointment and despair. We may try to convince ourselves that this is simply the way life is, that you can't have the good without the bad, there's no darkness without light, no yin without yang.

This is the essence of duality. We experience duality in this world of form. However, we don't need to play victim to the nature of duality. Keeping in mind the props and the stage are simply pixels on a screen—or information being interpreted by your consciousness as a physical universe with over eight billion human characters, not to mention all the critters that also play in this reality—the interpreted information is simply governed by a ruleset, i.e., chemistry, biology, and physics. This virtual reality appears to have duality and contrast everywhere. We have day and night, tall and short, large and small, clean and dirty, love and fear, etc.

Now let's pull back the curtain and look at the contrast that exists within consciousness, the aspect of reality that's fundamental, and the source that plays the characters in this virtual reality. Consciousness exists, and it either evolves or devolves based on the choices it makes. In theory, you could call this contrast. Evolution or devolution, order or chaos, low entropy or high entropy—within consciousness, these are the two states that are constantly contrasting each other.

Again, MBT has two assumptions:

1. Consciousness exists and
2. Evolution exists

Consciousness wants to evolve. It wants to grow and become more efficient. Evolution is the fundamental process within consciousness. It's in our nature to want to improve. This is built into our very being; it's at our core.

The reason for our existence is to evolve our consciousness, and we do this by making choices that come from love.

Chapter 6: Ego

I'd experienced a lot of adversity by the time I turned twenty-six. I like to think of my story as a mini rags-to-riches experience. In my early twenties, I ended an abusive relationship, overcame a serious drug addiction, made my way back into society, worked a legitimate job, and bought a home. This felt like an achievement for me, but once I reached the end goal, I got restless. I wanted more, but I didn't know what that *more* would be. So, I rented out my home, packed a bag, and headed to New York City.

It felt like the center of the universe. I loved it. I'm an introvert, but I tend to enjoy being immersed in a sea of people, experiencing the diversity and observing all the different worlds colliding together. It's like a collage of various life experiences woven together into one magnificent tapestry. I'm fascinated by people's stories.

The excitement of New York wore off after a few weeks, and I found myself wandering through the big city with no clear direction. I felt disconnected and alone. It's an odd thing, living in a city with over eight million people and feeling alone.

One night, I was window shopping on 5th Avenue, and I walked into a Barnes and Nobles to use the bathroom. After my bathroom stop, I took the escalator back down. As I descended, I noticed an orange book out of the corner of my eye. When I got off the escalator, I walked over to the shelf and picked it up. The title was *A New Earth* by Eckhart Tolle. *Never heard of him*, I thought. But for some reason, I had to buy the book.

I purchased the book, and it became my companion for the next few years. We spent a lot of time together. Tolle's concepts helped me learn more about myself, and they helped me understand the ego.

For the first time in my life, I started to notice the ego. In his book, *A New Earth*, Tolle explains that the ego is the voice in your head that you identify with. If you just thought, *What voice in my head?* It's that voice in your head, the one who asked. Who you really are is the awareness that observes the voice in your head.[4]

I continued to study the book. Six months later, I left NYC to pursue a rigorous physical training routine at a Muay Thai camp in Thailand. I brought the book to Asia with me, and I can clearly remember the transition I made from identifying with the voice in my head to observing the voice. I was in Phuket, Thailand, and it was my second month training at the camp. My days became routine: wake up, train for three hours, lunch, break, train for three more hours, swim, dinner, sleep, and repeat.

One morning, I woke up, and my thoughts started. *Okay, I need to get up now. I must train. I wonder if I should ride the scooter into camp or if I should jog. Maybe I…*

They were regular thoughts, but I was observing them and became annoyed. I was frustrated they were running on autopilot and that they were always there. It seemed like it was non-stop thinking. There were always thoughts in my head, and I couldn't seem to stop them.

"Shut up!" I finally yelled out loud. Silence.

But five seconds later, the thoughts were back. *Yeah, I'll take the scooter. That way I can ride to that really good pad thai place for lunch. Oh and…*

---

[4] Tolle, Eckhart. *A New Earth: Awakening to Your Life's Purpose.* Penguin, 2008.

It was an interesting phenomenon. I couldn't seem to control the thoughts. They just kept rambling like that friend with no social skills, the one who talks a lot and can't tell when no one is listening. On and on they went.

I continued to observe the ego and witness the thoughts. I did my best to get in touch with the awareness behind them, but it was challenging. After three months of Muay Thai, I decided to move to Northern Thailand and redirect my attention inwards through meditation. I lived in different Buddhist monasteries and tried to learn how to meditate. During my meditation practice, I noticed the thoughts were still there, but now, I was in a peaceful place as I tried observing the thoughts and not attaching to them. When I was attached to the thoughts, I tried to control them, which was exhausting. As soon as I let go of the control and allowed the thoughts to unfold, I became much less stressed. This allowed me to watch my thoughts, and they would often subside without my intervention.

This went on for a few months until I got bored and decided to go to the Philippines, where I stayed on a private island called Malapacao. I retreated to this island and immersed myself back into *A New Earth*. I thought maybe it would help if I learned more and used my thoughts to help me understand the purpose of life.

I learned a lot from that stage of my life. It gave me more awareness to work with, but I was still confused. I still had a lot of questions, and I still didn't understand what the purpose of this life was. I didn't completely understand the ego. From what I read of Tolle, the ego is our sense of self-identity. But don't we need an identity?

I took a three-day workshop with Eckhart's partner, Kim Eng, and I asked her, "Don't we need an ego to engage in this world of form? It would seem we need an identity to interact with people."

Kim replied, "No, we need to get rid of the ego." I was still confused.

I went on to learn more about the ego. But there are many ideas about what the ego is and how it functions, and it can be a highly charged subject. For this book, we'll use Tom's definition according to MBT: The ego is awareness in the service of fear.[5] When we get rid of our fear, we no longer have an ego. This gives us something practical to work with rather than getting lost in semantics and caught up in debates around what the ego is or isn't. Instead, we can apply ourselves toward doing the work to get rid of the fear and banish the ego. We don't need an ego to interact with one another; we can authentically engage with each other from a place of love.

MBT describes this journey toward ego abolishment. It's most commonly undertaken on one of three different paths:

1. Warriors Path
2. The Path of Surrender
3. The Path of Service

Most of us in the West tend to take the Warrior's Path. This is the toughest path, as it requires us to use our intellect to find our fears and insecurities and wrestle them to the ground. It can often feel like a battle in our minds and in our lives. We come up against a lot of hardships and obstacles, and it can weigh on us heavily as we try to fight our way through life.

The Path of Surrender is often found in the New Age scene. We hear advice like surrender to the present moment, accept the things you cannot change, go with the flow, and so forth. When we surrender to things as they are, we don't let our egos get in the way. Instead, we trust the process. Rather than trying to control and manipulate things to suit our needs, we simply allow life to naturally unfold.

Many religions and certain philosophies adhere to the path of service. A popular role model who walked this path was Mother Theresa. To walk this path is to live your life in service to others. Constantly giving to and helping others leaves you with no time to think about yourself or concern yourself with personal problems. Gandhi was also

---

[5] Campbell, Thomas. *My Big Toe: A Trilogy Unifying Philosophy, Physics, and Metaphysics: Awakening, Discovery, Inner Workings. Lightning Strike Books*, 2007.

an inspirational figure who said, "The best way to find yourself is to lose yourself in the service of others."[6]

In other words, lose the ego and find your best potential self. A life of service helps you actualize this potential. It would seem Einstein agreed when he said, "Only a life lived in service to others is a life worth living."

We often weave in and out of paths, but most of us have a dominant path: Warrior, Surrender or Service.

Which path are you on?

---

[6] "The best way to find yourself is to lose yourself in the service of others."—Define this quote by Mahatma Gandi." *Notes Editorial*, 28 Feb. 2012, https://www.enotes. com/homework-help/the-best-way-to-find-yourself-is-to-lose- yourself-405335. Accessed 23 Mar. 2023.

Chapter 7: Love is Letting Go of Fear

Repetition helps us learn new concepts. Because of this, let's revisit our purpose for existence according to MBT. We are individuated units of consciousness engaging in this world of form to evolve our consciousness and grow the quality of our being. In more scientific terms, we're here to lower our entropy. Or in a spiritual sense, we're here for spiritual evolution, liberation, and enlightenment.

Here we are, playing in this world of form, each of us doing our best to evolve who we are as individuals and collectively as a whole. We evolve ourselves by using free will to make wise decisions that lower our entropy and help us advance on our spiritual path.

We make choices that come from either fear or love. When we make a choice based on fear, we raise the entropy and create more chaos. When we make a choice from love, we lower the entropy and create more harmony.

When we're fearful, we become self-centered, and we do our best to take care of ourselves, protect what we have, fight for more of what we want, and do everything in our own best interests. We believe that if we don't take care of ourselves, no one will, and our reality turns into survival of the fittest, a dog-eat-dog world, every man for himself. This leads to nations creating division and fighting wars against one another, fearful of other countries trying to invade their territory or take over their resources. This mentality also leads to five percent of the population owning ninety percent of the wealth. This fear-based mentality has created the scarcity, poverty, war, destruction, and chaos we experience in our reality today.

What we're experiencing in our world is a social system in a high-entropy state with everyone competing against one another, people fighting and killing each other, and individuals using scare tactics to manipulate others into doing what they want them to do. A high-entropy system is produced by a civilization overcome by fear, and it's inefficient.

On the other hand, a low-entropy system is one that works very well. It's extremely efficient, and it produces positive results. A low-entropy system can only be created by the absence of fear. When we're no longer afraid, we let our guard down, and we don't feel the need to protect what we have because we're not afraid of losing anything. Instead, we learn to trust one another.

Without fear, we stop worrying about not having enough. Instead, we learn to appreciate what we have, and we begin to share our resources. We become less self-centered, and we shift our attention toward helping each other. Without fear, we no longer worry about our personal problems, and we stop stressing over how we're going to take care of ourselves. We start redirecting our attention toward others. We open our hearts and start looking at ways we can be more helpful, cooperative, and caring toward others. When we realize all our struggles, concerns, problems, and dilemmas stem from fear, we can start doing the work to help us take responsibility and let go of the fear.

A social system that has eradicated most of its fear becomes a society that works together and has compassion for one another. When we all have the intention of lifting each other up, supporting one another, and helping each other succeed, there's no limit to the type of paradise we can create. Our social, economic, educational, and political systems will change once we, the people, change. Our systems are simply reflections of us.

The best thing we, the individual (IUOC), can do is change ourselves. This isn't a new concept. Most of us are familiar with a quote famously attributed to Gandhi: "We must be the change we wish to see in the world."[7]

This isn't just the best thing one can do; it's the *only* thing we can do. We can't change other people. We can only change ourselves. This is precisely what each of us came here to do. We can walk around aimlessly, manifesting and manipulating form in this physical matter reality, or we can align with our purpose. The choice is ours.

To be clear, there's no shame in wandering through the world, drifting through life, and exploring new adventures. In fact, this can be a lot of fun. I did this for most of my life, and it *was* fun—and scary at times. It's kind of like going through a haunted house or riding a roller coaster. You know it's going to be scary, but that's part of the fun. Choosing to ride the roller coaster is a metaphor for life. MBT shows us that we continue to incarnate into different experience packets (lifetimes) to help us move forward with the evolution of our consciousness.

According to MBT, the IUOCs that have had many life experience packets and have significantly evolved their consciousness need to home in on key elements. They have specific things to work on, and these parts of our consciousness will incarnate into a more scripted life plan. Certain esoteric teachings describe this as a "soul contract" that the soul will be inspired to follow when they come to this reality.

The newer units of our consciousness that aren't as experienced will come into this reality for any type of experience. These pieces of our consciousness don't need any specific lessons. Just incarnating into this reality will help these units gain new experiences and provide them with opportunities to make choices and potentially evolve.

Going back to the roller coaster metaphor, we remember the difficulties we've faced in this reality, but we realize these challenges, although dangerous at times, also create a lot of variety, surprise, and

---

[7] *The Collected Works of Mahatma Gandhi (Electronic Book).* vol. 13, *Publications Division Government of India,* 1999.

excitement. Like stepping into the coaster cart, we incarnate into a new avatar, buckle up, and enjoy the ride.

Growing up and evolving is precisely why we're here. When one piece of our consciousness evolves, it helps all of us because we're connected through consciousness. Relating back to Chapter 2, we're all part of the LCS (larger consciousness system). The more IUOCs that grow up, the more we evolve as a collective. But we don't have to wait for the masses to evolve before experiencing the benefits of evolved consciousness. When you focus your intent on making low-entropy decisions that come from love, absent of fear, you'll start noticing positive changes showing up in your life.

As you begin to evolve, your own personal journey becomes a lot lighter. Things just seem to flow better. You'll notice a sense of ease and joy that permeates through all your experiences. Your hard work won't go unnoticed, and the more you focus your intent on growing up and evolving, the more happiness, freedom, and beauty you'll invite into your world.

The larger consciousness system wants you to succeed because, as you evolve, it evolves. The larger consciousness system helps us to evolve, and when you're serious about growing up, the LCS will give you special help. It puts its resources where they're most beneficial. You'll attract more help when you are serious about evolving.

So how do we let go of fear?

As I mentioned before, the most important thing you can do is have a clear intention. Your intention to let go of fear must come from the being level. It must be your honest, committed intent to grow up. With this strong, steady, and clear intent, you can begin the process of removing fear.

1. Pay attention to your feelings. When you're aware of a negative emotion, trace it back to a fear and own that fear.
2. Feel the fear. Be courageous and move through it.
3. Repeat.

Yes, it's that simple. I realize you may want a process that's laid out for you and guarantees that, as long as you follow steps one through five, you'll reach a state of self-actualization. I hate to disappoint you, but it doesn't work that way. As I mentioned earlier, the most important thing you can do is have a strong intent, a persistent motivation to grow the quality of your consciousness by making low-entropy decisions.

When you make growing up your number one priority and focus on making low-entropy decisions, you'll start to notice how all your choices drive the quality of your consciousness. Every decision you make will either pull you toward evolution and a lower state of entropy or push you away into a higher state of entropy filled with anger, stress, greed, or any other negative emotion. That's the beauty of evolution in this physical matter reality. We have countless opportunities to evolve ourselves, improve the quality of our being, and lower our entropy.

This all sounds well and good, but what about when our circumstances aren't well and good? It's easy to talk about letting go of fear on paper, but when we're actually *living* that fear, things get a lot harder. The thing to remember is that our circumstances are never the deciding factor. What matters is how we choose to respond. Stop paying so much attention to the event itself and start paying more attention to how you're showing up, how you're choosing to react, and what emotions you're experiencing—without giving in to the need to blame others.

I became angry the other day, and rather than getting furious, I decided to get curious. I asked myself, *Why am I choosing to feel this way?* The first few times I asked myself this question, I blamed the other individual. Then I reminded myself I'm never upset for the reason I think. This helped me dig a little deeper.

Okay, I'm not upset because of the situation itself. I'm allowing the situation to trigger a fear hidden deep inside me. This attitude encourages the fear to surface to the light of conscious awareness so I can face it and move through it, which will help me to let it go. This process sometimes takes me days, depending on the intensity of the emotion.

Although the process may seem simple, try it yourself and watch what happens. If you're anything like me, your ego will keep coming up in sneaky little ways to try to convince you the reason you're feeling upset is anything but your fear. Remember, our ego is awareness in the service of fear.

In most cases, our fear is neatly tucked away, hiding in the trenches, and our ego speaks on its behalf. It's our ego that says, *It's his fault I feel so awful. How dare he talk to me like that? He's such a jerk. What a loser! I'm better off without him.* It's our ego that blames everyone else and never takes the time to reveal what's really going on inside of us.

When we take the time to see what's really going on, we'll notice our fear is the actual cause of all life's misery. Rather than blaming someone else for your misery, take a moment and see if you can dig a little deeper. Ask yourself, *Why am I choosing to get upset by this?* Perhaps it's because what he said triggered my fear about not being lovable or my fear of inadequacy. Maybe his words triggered something inside me I need to pay attention to and look at.

Again, this process will require some patience and a whole lot of honesty. This is usually around the point where the ego pipes up and says, *Well, if he wasn't such a jerk face, then I wouldn't feel like I'm inadequate because he said…*

Then we go to the second stage of the process. Remind yourself that you're never upset for the reasons you think.

Okay, fine. Maybe I'm not upset by his words. Maybe there's something deeper upsetting me.

This helps us start the self-inquiry process that can last minutes, hours, days, weeks, years, or even lifetimes, depending on the strength of your intent to evolve the quality of your consciousness. If your intent is weak and wavering, you'll take the easy way out of this process and continue blaming others for your misery. If your intent is strong, steady, and clear, you'll grow up. It takes patience and perseverance, but know that you're well on your way.

Another helpful tip to interrupt the pattern is to ask in your head or out loud, *So what, now what?* When you keep playing the story over in your head, stop yourself and ask, *So what?* Yes, this event happened. *Now what am I going to do about it?* You can either continue running the story over in your head and keep making yourself upset, or you can drop the story, learn from the situation, and move on.

Instead of moving forward, we often get stuck in the victim story. We tell ourselves, *I can't do this because I'm too old, too short, too fat, too thin...* You fill in the blank. We convince ourselves we're not good enough, and we find evidence to support it. Or we play the victim story of how so-and-so did us wrong.

I remember the first time I used this, *So what, now what?* tool. It was extremely efficient at helping me to interrupt the old pattern and rewrite a new story.

I was lying in bed, thinking about my ex-husband, and telling myself how awful he was. I was finding evidence to prove it, and in the midst of this, I thought, *So what?* It was quite refreshing, actually. It was liberating to break the old pattern of victimhood.

So what if he did that, I thought. *Are you just going to sit here and play your story over and over again and generate negativity and animosity toward him? Or are you going to change your story and stop playing the victim?*

So what if that happened? *Now what* am I going to do about it?

Now I'm going to learn from it. That's what I'm going to do. I'm going to learn discernment, compassion, and resilience.

It takes a strong and steady intent to evolve. But with the desire to do so, we will find the way. However, we must be committed to growth if we want to see it, and once we find it, we'll also see that fear is the problem and love is the answer.

Chapter 8: Fear is Ignorance Trapped in a Little Picture

WHEN I STARTED WRITING THIS chapter, I was at a ten-day vipassana meditation camp. Ten days of silence, no talking, reading, or writing. Only meditating and eating two modest meals a day. I broke the rule and snuck in my laptop. And I continued writing because that's how I roll.

On day four of the camp, I was seven weeks pregnant with my third child. During the night, I had sharp stomach cramps, and the morning after, I started spotting. As soon as I noticed this, the first thought that entered my mind was, *Oh, thank god I'm not stuck with this guy.* Then I shook my head and thought, *Wow. Is this how I really feel about my relationship?*

This threw me off, and I quickly reminded myself that there was an unborn child's life at stake. I immediately felt fear come up. My fear manifested itself in the form of sadness and tears. I felt the fear of losing my unborn child. I then started worrying, and I decided to leave the camp early to check in with my midwife. As I waited to speak with the manager at the meditation camp, I started to look at my fear and asked myself if I could let go of it.

The fear of losing an unborn child feels very real. But I pulled myself out of my little-picture perspective and stopped thinking of how devastated I would be. I did my best to see a big-picture perspective.

When I looked at this situation immersed in my life experience as Vanessa, all I could think about was myself, how terrible this would be for *me*, how sad I would be, how depressing this would be for *me*. The fear was all about me. Then an interesting thing happened. When I had this realization, I felt a gentle insight from within telling me to stay. And with that small sign from my intuition, I decided to stay and write this.

I remembered another piece of wisdom I'd heard from Tom: "The being level simply nudges you. It doesn't try to convince you with logic or reason."

What is a big-picture perspective versus a little-picture perspective?

A little picture is one obscured by fear. When we start letting go of fear, we expand our vision, and we broaden our understanding. We open up to more insight, and we increase our decision space. MBT describes decision space as the number of choices or opportunities available.

In the example of my situation, I was viewing the experience from a fear-based perspective. I was overwhelmed by the fear of having a miscarriage, and the only decision I could see was to leave. When faced with fight or flight, I chose flight.

However, once I took a moment to remove the fear, I widened my decision space, and more choices appeared before me. I could stay and write about the experience. I could go to a nearby clinic to make sure our baby was okay. I could call the health line. I could email my midwife, or I could stay at the meditation camp and trust my intuition that everything would be okay.

When we have a big-picture perspective, we realize that it's not the events or the situations that matter. It's how we decide to deal with our circumstances that's important. There's a myriad of unique, challenging, and trying experiences happening to each of us every second of every day. We're having these experiences so we can respond to them, deal with them, and make choices that help us evolve the quality of our consciousness.

I decided to stay at the meditation camp and call the health line. They advised me to see a doctor. I immediately went to the local emergency room, and the doctor gave me an ultrasound. He started explaining what he was seeing, leaning toward the idea that I may be having a miscarriage.

I asked him, "Does this happen often?" He paused and looked at me.

I searched his eyes for an answer and asked again. "Do you see this a lot? Do many women have miscarriages?"

"Well," he said, "to be honest…" Then he got up and walked over to another doctor.

He didn't have to finish his answer. I knew the answer was, yes, miscarriages happen all the time.

It wasn't the miscarriage itself that I should have been focused on. It was my reaction to the miscarriage, how I chose to respond to the experience.

With all this weighing on my mind, the doctor told me to go to a clinic in another town. This clinic had more advanced technology, and they would be able to give me a more accurate diagnosis. The doctor didn't want to tell me anything without an accurate ultrasound. I called the meditation center and told them what the doctor said before I made my way over to the second clinic.

While I was waiting in the lobby for my results, I saw an older couple who looked to be in their nineties, waiting to see a doctor. The wife wheeled her husband up to the front desk, and the lady at the front asked for the husband's ID. "One second," said the wife. "Let me go get it in my purse." Then she walked back over to the chairs where her purse was.

The front desk lady asked the old man for an emergency contact number. The man called out to his wife, "Honey, do you know Bill's number?"

"Yes, sweetie. Let me look it up for you." The wife smiled at her husband as she walked back to the counter and opened her purse.

"Okay," the man said to the front desk lady. "My wife will get the phone number for you." He looked up at her adoringly.

I watched this couple in awe. Here were two people who took care of each other, respected each other, and loved each other unconditionally. My eyes welled up as I witnessed their love for one another.

Ah, I thought. *So this is a loved-based relationship. This is what it looks like. It's beautiful.*

"Vanessa Wideski," a nurse called. "The doctor will see you now."

I got up and followed the nurse into the doctor's room. The doctor told me it was too early to see if I'd had a miscarriage and I would have to wait until further along to find out for sure. It seemed like she was trying to stay neutral, but I could tell by her tone that she was hinting on the side of miscarriage.

I thanked her for her time and drove back to the meditation camp.

When I arrived at the camp, the manager advised me to go home. They thought that, due to my situation, it was best that I leave. I nodded in agreement, and the manager commented on how calm I'd been during this turn in events. But when I think about it, there's no better place this could have happened. Being in a meditation camp, zenned out, calm as a cucumber and cool as ice was probably the best place to receive unwanted news.

During the nine-hour drive home, I listened to some of Tom's talks, and I found that listening to the MBT insights really helped me put things in perspective and see a bigger picture. It helped me be more accountable to myself and interrupt the victim pattern I'd made a habit of perpetuating.

In case you're unfamiliar with the victim pattern, it looks like this:

How could this happen to me? Why me?

Nobody gets me.

What about meee…

Ah yes, the victim. We love to play the victim because it excuses us from having to do any work ourselves. If nothing is my fault, I don't have to change. I can just blame everyone else for my bad behavior.

We can learn a lot about ourselves when we're aware of our emotions, thoughts, and reactions. From my limited point of view, I cut myself off from experiencing anything other than the negative emotions that came from fear. It's my fear that limits me from seeing reality in any way other than what I'm experiencing. It's my fear that keeps me trapped in a narrow-minded perspective.

Fear makes us self-centered. This fear-based, scarcity mentality causes us to view reality through a narrow perspective of *what's in it for me?* and *how will I benefit from this?* Every time something doesn't work out the way we want it to, we get upset because it's not helping *me* get ahead. It's causing me harm. Poor me. Woe is me.

The other day, I was sitting in my car, my kids in the backseat. We were parked in the driveway, and I was lost in thought, feeling upset and depressed about my relationship with my boyfriend at the time.

My three-year-old daughter, Nala, looked at me through the rear-view mirror. She blinked her big brown eyes and asked me her signature question that's become famous throughout our family: "Mommy, are you happy?"

I smiled and thought for a moment. "No, honey," I said as tears welled up in my eyes. "I'm actually feeling really sad."

To this, she gave me a curious look and said, "Oh wait, can you take this off?" She pointed to her seatbelt.

I turned to the back of the car and unbuckled her seatbelt. She scooted up to the front of the car and sat beside me in the passenger seat. She looked up at me again with those innocent, brown eyes and asked, "Why are you sad, Mommy?"

I pondered the question and thought, *Because things aren't working out the way I want them to.* This made me smile as I realized what I was doing. I was stuck in my little picture, only thinking about myself. I remembered that, in the bigger picture, it doesn't matter what happens to us. All that's important is how we deal with what happens to us.

As long as we're doing our best to learn and grow from our life experiences, we're on the fast track to spiritual progress. A helpful question I often ask myself during highly emotional times is, *What do I need to learn from this?*

I'm doing my best to make this a habit. Every time I find myself reacting from a place of fear (i.e., acting out of anger, feeling frustrated, annoyed, impatient, or anything other than content), I simply ask myself, *What do I need to learn from this?* Rather than paying attention to the event itself, this question prompts me to see a bigger picture.

What did I need to learn from feeling sad about my relationship with my partner?

I needed to learn how to accept people as they are and walk away from people who can't accept me for who I am. I also had to learn that things don't always turn out the way we plan, and that's okay. I learned how to let go of control and instead allow life to unfold in a natural way.

When we learn to see our negative emotions as little gifts that point us in the direction we need to go, we start to create a new positive habit. Previously, when a negative emotion would arise, my first instinct was to suppress the emotion. Like so many others, I was raised to believe that negative emotions were wrong, vulnerability was weak, and only the strong survived. Many of us have been taught that big girls/boys don't cry, and we need to suck it up and move on. In the past, if I felt sad, I wouldn't admit it. I would hide it and distract myself with alcohol, food, internet, gossip, or anything that would redirect my focus away from my emotions.

It was unthinkable to cry in front of my friends. Even as a child, if I fell in the playground, my parents encouraged me not to cry. Crying was a sign of weakness.

This is no fault of my parents. They were doing the best they could. They raised me based on their own beliefs and what they thought was best for me. That meant raising a strong, independent child who would grow up, learn to take care of herself, and not let others take advantage of her. They wanted to raise me with confidence. Isn't that what most parents want—self-sufficient kids who believe in themselves and are confident in who they are?

The only problem with this approach is that most of us have no idea who we are. Many of us believe that we're the image of ourselves we've created. We feel as though our personalities are the entirety of who we are. Most of us are out of touch with our authentic self because we hide behind our ego. Rather than having a strong sense of self-worth and connecting with who we truly are, we build up a strong ego, and we identify with who we think we should be. Once we become aware of this, we begin the journey home to ourselves, our true selves.

When we let go of our fears, we become more aligned with our core, authentic selves. By shifting our focus from our ego, we're able to see the bigger picture. When we no longer have an ego to manage and worry about, we gain the energy and awareness to see that bigger picture, instead of being trapped in a small, egoic picture.

Chapter 9: Fear Shrinks, Love Grows

WHEN IT'S ABOUT ME, I'M coming from fear. When it's about others, I'm coming from love.

Let me explain how this works: fear makes us feel as though we need to protect ourselves from others. For example, if I have a fear of inadequacy and I feel like I'm not good enough, I create an ego that tries to keep me safe. The ego I create will either overcompensate for my lack of confidence and I'll come across as arrogant, or I'll create an ego that tries to blend in, not wanting to draw attention from others so they won't find out how inadequate I am.

It's much easier to notice this in others than to recognize it in ourselves. Think of a friend or a family member who brags all the time. They constantly talk about how great they are and show off the new toys they've accumulated. Or on the flip side, think about a talented friend who has great ideas but never seems to speak up and share their ideas with others.

Why do you think these people do this? Is it because the friend who brags is so confident in themselves they need to prove it to the world? Is the friend who never shares their ideas doing so because they're super confident and don't need to talk to others about their creative insights? Perhaps, but the more likely reasons are the friend who brags about themselves and shows off their toys wants to feel good about themselves. They're looking for acceptance and validation from others. The friend who doesn't speak up is often afraid of how others will perceive them. They may be fearful of rejection, disapproval, or ridicule.

How do you react when your friends, family members, colleagues, or anyone you know starts bragging or being conceited? What feelings come up for you? Do you find yourself getting frustrated with this person or feeling angry, hurt, or disappointed in any way? Really feel the emotions that come up when you identify someone like this.

For me, this person is my father. He brags about his kids all the time, all four of us. The feeling that comes up for me is embarrassment. But why am I embarrassed?

I'm never upset for the reasons I think.

My feeling of embarrassment has nothing to do with my father's words or actions. Anything he does or says is neutral unless I attach a meaning to it and choose to have an emotional response. The emotional response I have *is mine.*

Once I own the emotion and take responsibility for it, I can do the work needed to grow up. But if I continue to blame others, I'll never change. This feeling of embarrassment comes from me, from my being. I have fear at the being level that I need to accept and work through.

The first step in working through my fears is acknowledgement. First, I need to acknowledge that I have fear. I must admit that my fear exists.

The path of least resistance would dismiss these fears. In the example with my dad, it's easy for me to say, "If your dad bragged about you and your siblings all the time, you would be embarrassed too."

My friends might even agree with me. "Oh, yeah. You're right. I would be embarrassed too. That's *so* embarrassing."

Other friends may offer a different perspective. "He's just being a proud father. There's nothing wrong with that." But whether or not I'm willing to see another perspective depends on how much fear I have.

As I pointed out several times (and will continue to point out because repetition is key), it's never the event or situation that matters. It's our reaction to the situation. My dad and his bragging aren't the cause of my embarrassment. What's causing me to feel embarrassed is my fear of inadequacy that I keep hidden away from everyone, including myself. If I didn't have a fear of inadequacy, if I was beaming with love and compassion for all of humankind and had an abundance of confidence in myself, do you think I would feel embarrassed…ever? No. Of course not! I would only feel love, peace, and joy. When I let go of fear, I remove my insecurities, and when I'm free of insecurities, there's nothing left to get triggered. Instead, I respond with love.

When we break it down like this, we see that it's futile to try to fix anything outside of ourselves. The only thing that requires work is you and me. When we work on letting go of our fear, we become more loving. We let go of our fears by facing them and accepting them. If I continue to blame my dad for making me feel embarrassed, I'll remain stuck in my fear.

By being accountable and owning my feelings, I start to let go of the fear, and I can consider a new perspective. Continuing with the example of my dad, it may look like this:

Okay, maybe my dad is just being a proud father. Sure, I get that. He's proud of his kids. I can accept him for who he is because I know he's doing the best he can.

I've been practicing this for a few years with my father, and the first few times I heard him bragging about his kids, I continued to feel embarrassed. But as I continued to apply this new perspective over time, my embarrassment transformed into compassion.

In this example, I was making it about me. I was worried about how others would judge me *(Oh my god, what are they going to think of me and my crazy, bragging father?)*, and that's why I felt embarrassed. When I shifted the focus onto others—for example, when I put my attention onto my dad—I could empathize with him and see where he's coming from, and it brought me to a place of compassion and acceptance. I shifted my awareness, opened myself up to a broader level of understanding, and expanded my perspective.

I recently called my dad to catch up and see how he was doing. At the end of our conversation, I mentioned I was writing a book. He asked me what it was about, and I told him it was called *My Big EGO, a Practical Application of My Big TOE.* I waited for him to respond, and after a couple seconds of dead air on the phone, he said, "I'm gonna brag so hard!"

I just laughed and replied with, "Thanks, Pop. You'll be my biggest fan."

When I make it about me, I'm coming from fear. When I make it about others, I'm coming from love. Everyone wins when we make it about others—including you. I was feeling embarrassed because I was stuck in my little picture. If I make it about others and put my focus on my father, not only do I feel better by feeling compassion rather than embarrassment, but my father also wins too. Instead of rolling my eyes and walking away from him, I can simply send him love and accept him just as he is.

When we're stuck in our story, stuck in a limited perspective, it can be difficult to see the light. If we're wrapped up in negativity and can't seem to find a way out of it, we need to ask ourselves, *Am I making this about myself?* If so, then we're coming from fear and trapped in our own little pictures.

Here's a fun visual my friend Angelita taught me. Every time you catch yourself making it about you, visualize yourself doing the robot dance and repeat, "It's not about me, it's not about me, it's not about me." Not only will you interrupt the pattern, you'll give yourself something to chuckle about. Hopefully, this will snap you out of your fear.

Fear is paralyzing at times. It keeps us stuck in old patterns and beliefs. Fear prevents us from trying anything new. Fear is stifling.

Let's go back to the argument that we need fear because it keeps us safe. An example I hear often is, "If we're young and burn ourselves on the stove, we become afraid of the stove, and this fear prevents us from burning ourselves again. Fear protects us from doing dangerous things like walking alone in the woods at night and getting attacked by a bear."

If we look closer at these examples, we can conclude that most of us would be scared if we came across a bear in the woods at night or if we burned our hand on the stove as a young child. However, it's not the fear that prevents us from getting attacked by a bear or burning our hand on a stove. It's intelligence that helps us navigate this world without getting injured. Our intellect is a marvelous tool that can help us in this physical reality frame. Intelligence informs us of the dangers that come from touching a hot stove and walking into the woods alone at night. Our intelligence helps keep us safe. Fear doesn't keep us safe. In fact, fear has the opposite effect.

If we see a bear and we are fearful, we may run away, and the bear may chase us. If, on the other hand, we remove the fear and stay calm, our intelligence will inform us to wave our arms around, get big, and make a lot of noise. If we're overcome by fear, we won't be able to think straight and may end up doing something that causes us more harm than good. Fear is never the answer.

"Okay," you say. "Sure, that makes sense. But what are the chances of running into a bear?" And you're right. You have a higher chance of experiencing fatal anaphylactic shock from a bee sting than you do from a bear attack.[8] But the most common fears we face are the subtle fears: the fear of rejection, the fear of abandonment, the fear of failure, and the fear of inadequacy.

I've found the fear of inadequacy to be the most common fear. But once we remove it, we no longer feel driven to be in constant competition with the world. We don't have a desire to take others down so we can feel better. When we remove the fear that we aren't good enough, we stop trying to control people and manipulate events to meet our needs and make us feel better.

You may be thinking, *This isn't me. I don't try to take people down to feel good about myself.* Ask yourself, have you ever complained about another

---

[8] Arnold, Carrie. "Why You're More Likely To Be Killed By a Bee Than a Bear." *National Geographic*, 10 Aug. 2015, www.nationalgeographic.com/animals/article/150810-grizzly-bears-attack-yellowstone-animals. Accessed 23 Mar. 2023.

individual? Have you ever judged someone in a negative light? Have you ever found yourself saying or thinking any of the following: *Oh my gosh, what is he/she/they wearing? What's wrong with this person? Why are they so slow?* Or even, *He/she/they are being so selfish stupid/boring/mean/fake/egotistical…* You fill in the blank.

Most of us make negative judgments from time to time, and the reason we complain or put others down is because, on a subtle and superficial level, it makes us feel better about ourselves. *So-and-so is such a show-off. Good thing I'm not like her. I'm better than that.* This is what we're insinuating. Why else would we put others down? We've been brought up in a culture that thrives on rank and classifications: lower class, middle class, and upper class. We're conditioned to see where we fit in, and consequently, we judge others to see where they fit in and how we rank in comparison to them.

Maybe you're a rarity, and you don't judge others. Do you ever find yourself saying or thinking statements like *the government is so moronic* or *the education system is terrible*? Do you ever find yourself judging or condemning systems or groups? The same idea applies here. It's less noticeable, but it implies the same thing while hiding under the guise of being plugged in.

When we condemn or put other people, places, or things down, we're not helping the situation. We're simply trying to make ourselves temporarily feel better from an intellectual and superficial level. We're trying to tell ourselves, *I'm better than that,* but you never look good trying to make someone else look bad.

The very thing we put down is simply a reflection of our consciousness. Remember, we're all connected from a big-picture perspective. We're one unified field of information or consciousness. If you see another individuated unit of consciousness committing acts of atrocity and you condemn them, remind yourself that person—the IUOC playing that person—has been through different experiences than you. That IUOC is doing the best they can based on their current level of understanding, which has been formed by all their past challenges, adversities, and lifetimes of experiences. This is compassion. This is unconditional love.

To quote Eckhart Tolle, "Love is the recognition of oneness in a world of duality."[9]

I've heard Tom Campbell share a similar sentiment: "When you feel connected, everyone is important.

You care about all people, animals, and critters."

The more we understand the big picture, the more it helps us grow.

When we're wrapped in the grips of fear and only thinking about ourselves, it becomes difficult to see a bigger picture. By removing the fear, we stop trying to protect ourselves, and we start looking outside our little picture. We start seeing others for who they are, and we begin to open to a bigger understanding. This is how we cultivate compassion for others. When we move away from thinking about ourselves and start empathizing with others, we notice a lightness that permeates our daily interactions. We stop taking things so personally, and we begin to see more perspectives.

It's quite astonishing if you think about it. Nearly every time we get upset or experience a negative emotion, it's because we're only thinking about ourselves. I can think of one example that may challenge this statement, and that's feeling a negative emotion upon witnessing or hearing someone else's experience. For example, when others share a sad experience with us, we tend to empathize with them and feel sadness too. In this case, however, we often feel sadness because we're putting ourselves in the other person's shoes. We think, *What if that happened to me?* We imagine the situation happening in our own lives, which is, again, me-focused.

I'm still experimenting with this idea. However, I feel that true empathy is understanding where the other person is coming from without having to experience the depth of their feelings because no one will ever know what it truly feels like to be you, me, or anyone else. The only one who can fully experience your feelings is you.

---

[9] Tolle, Eckhart. *A New Earth: Awakening to Your Life's Purpose. Penguin*, 2008.

I like to look at empathy as a form of compassion where I can do my best to understand a person's situation and connect with them on a deeper level. Empathy is being able to tune into another person's feelings and recognize their emotional state so you can help them. I don't think of empathy as feeling the other person's feelings because, as I mentioned, we'll never know what it's like to be another person. However, we can relate to others. We can share similar feelings, we can understand their feelings, and we can help them work through their feelings without having to take on their emotions ourselves.

Because we're connected through consciousness, we can pick up on what others are feeling. We might get a sample or a taste of what someone feels, but we won't get the whole enchilada unless we've walked in that person's shoes. We *will* get information on the surface level, and this information may come in the form of an emotion. Then we interpret that emotion. Some of us will interpret those feelings as our own. Others will know who the emotion comes from but will still interpret the emotion based on their own experiences.

I've experimented with this concept while watching movies, and I encourage you to play around with it too. When you watch a sad scene—let's say a mother losing a child—if you find yourself feeling sad, ask yourself why. Is it because the woman on the screen lost her only daughter? Why is that sad for you? The woman on the screen isn't real. The child is a fictional character, and yet we still cry and feel sad. I'm learning to understand that I feel sadness because I imagine the event happening to me. I make it about me, and that's why I experience the negative emotion.

When I first met Tom at the Monroe Institute (TMI) in 2015, I didn't know it at the time, but I had a lot of insecurities and suppressed fear. I was attending a six-day immersive course where we spent our days listening to binaural beats inside something called a check unit and explored altered states of consciousness. Binaural beats are audio files that help train our brainwaves to induce a deep, meditative state. The check unit is similar to a bunker, a completely enclosed bed with a blackout curtain acting as the entrance and exit. Inside each check unit is a switch that turns on a light in the main lab room. A program facilitator monitors the lab, watching the switches and controlling the binaural beats. When participants are ready in their check units, they switch their lights off, and when the facilitator sees that everyone is ready, they know to start the binaural beats.

On my third day at the Monroe Institute, we were all given an energy healing exercise. The other participants and I retreated to our check units, put on our headphones, then flipped our switches to begin the exercise.

What happened next was unexpected. My son and daughter came to mind, and I had strong feelings of love for them. After a few minutes of this, I started feeling guilty for being away from them. The next thing I knew, I was crying and feeling like an awful mother for leaving my children. I spent the whole exercise, in my check unit, crying and telling myself I would spend more time with my kids. The session came to an end, and through the headphones, I heard, "Our session is over. Let your light shine."

I flipped the switch, took off my headphones, and lay in my check unit. *Oh, man*, I thought. *I don't want to go downstairs.*

After each session, all the participants regrouped in the main room to share our experiences and ask questions. This part of the course was interesting because it gave us the opportunity to listen to everyone's experiences and to share our own. It was a comfortable space. The program facilitator put out fresh snacks, and there was often tea, coffee, juice, and other refreshments. It felt like we were hanging out in good a friend's living room.

But for this exercise, I didn't want to go into the main room to join Tom and the other participants. I lay there in my check unit with damp cheeks and red eyes. *Ugh, I don't want to cry in front of everyone. I just want to stay here.*

Then I felt an internal nudge. *Go join in. You don't have to talk. Just listen. Fine*, I said to myself.

Still resistant, I got up, wiped my face, and slowly made my way downstairs. I noticed that most of the participants were already seated in the main room. I would normally grab snacks and sit up front, but this time, I walked into the room with my head down, trying not to make eye contact with anyone as I found a seat in the back corner.

I sensed that Tom was looking at me. It felt like he was observing me with curiosity and wonder. I remained silent throughout the session, afraid that as soon as I opened my mouth, I would start sobbing, a big, ugly cry with snot bubbles and dry heaves.

I shifted back and forth from listening to the thoughts in my head to listening to the conversation. I took copious notes, and by the end of the session, I was feeling a lot better. I didn't have to ask any questions out loud. Tom answered all my inquiries throughout the session. He seemed to have a knack for being highly in tune with how we were feeling and what we were thinking.

I struggled to understand my emotions, so I asked Tom about sadness, and he shared that sadness can be an aspect of love. When you witness a sad event happening to someone and you see that person experiencing pain, you may feel sad when there's nothing you can do to take that pain away. This sadness is compassion and love for the person you care about. This explanation helped me further my understanding of emotions. I was curious to understand my emotions because Tom explained that your emotions come from your being level. They are your real self. I could see that being in touch with my emotions would help me let go of my fear and come from a powerful place of love.

When we come from love and make it about others, we immediately think about how we can help that person or make them feel better. Using the example of a mother losing a child, if we are overcome by grief, how can we be of any service to the mother? How can we help the mother manage her emotions if we cannot manage our own? By letting go of our own fears, we can help others more effectively. In this case, the best way to help the mother is by offering your love and support and gently helping her see a bigger picture. Connect with her and stay positive. She's overcome with sadness and grief. She doesn't need anyone else to add to it. She needs positive energy; she needs love and compassion. When we are loving and compassionate to others, it helps them come to a better place.

Have you ever been in a situation with someone who was mad or upset with you? I often have. I've had instances where I've been reactive. I've responded with anger and gotten defensive. But I'm learning to respond with love.

I'll be the first to admit that this can be challenging at times, especially in a relationship with a significant other. For me, relationships are the ultimate classroom where the big tests are given. I'm learning to respond with love when my significant other directs his anger toward me. Instead of reacting, taking it personally, and coming from fear, I take a moment, breathe, and respond with love. When I practice this, I feel better, and it transforms his anger, bringing him to a better place himself. It's quite magical, and though it sounds simple and easy to apply, it can be difficult the first few times. But once you start practicing this on a regular basis, it becomes a habitual process. Responding with love becomes your new baseline.

I'll always remember the first time I really applied this concept in a tough situation. My friend, Darren, was facilitating workshops for a personal development company, and one day, he and I were chatting over coffee when I asked him what he taught in these workshops. He enthusiastically shared his experience with the company and told me how they changed his life.

"Interesting," I said. "Maybe my boyfriend (we'll call him Dan) should take a workshop." Clearly, I didn't need to do any work, but my boyfriend—oh, *lordy*, he needed help.

A few days later, I invited Dan to learn more about the workshop, and he agreed to do it with me. The following month, we showed up for the three-day course. Everyone opened up, and people shared their stories of trauma. There were tears, and it was an honest weekend filled with authenticity and vulnerability. I enjoy this type of interaction, and Dan seemed to be having a good time as well.

On the final evening of the course, everyone formed a giant circle around the room as soft music played in the background. The doors at the back of the room opened, and in came our friends and family to surprise us with flowers and hugs. My friend Darren walked over to me, handed me flowers, and gave me a hug.

"What did you think?" he asked. "It was incredible!" I said.

Before I could go on, I noticed Jeff, my ex-boyfriend, and a friend of Darren's walking over. "Hey, how are you?" Jeff asked as he leaned over to give me a hug.

Darren excused himself and walked over to give my current boyfriend, Dan, a hug and a card. I resisted making eye contact with Dan because I could already feel his anger. I knew Dan was upset that Jeff was in the room, and I could feel him glaring at me.

I answered Jeff and told him I was doing well. I could still feel Dan's razor stare, and I did my best to shield myself from his negativity. I wanted to be polite to my friends, and I didn't want Dan's anger and jealousy to interfere with how I was feeling. But at the same time, I cared for Dan, and I was feeling incredibly concerned for him. Jeff and I had ended our six-month relationship on great terms. We remained close friends, and two weeks after ending that relationship, I'd met Dan. But ever since Dan and I had started dating, I'd avoided Jeff because our friendship bothered him.

So yeah. This was kind of awkward.

Jeff asked if Dan and I wanted to go out with them for drinks after, and I told him I'd ask Dan. I braced myself and looked over in Dan's direction, but he was already gone.

Of course he is, I thought.

I said goodbye to a few people and left the room to look for Dan. I spotted one of the participants from our workshop, walked over to her, and asked if she knew where Dan was.

She looked at me and said, "Girl, he's pissed."

I sighed. "Yeah, I'm not looking forward to putting out this fire. Where'd he go?" "I think he went to his truck to leave," she said with a shrug.

I walked out to his truck. He was sitting in the driver's seat, blazing on his vape pen. There we were,

Dan sitting in the driver's seat of his white F-150, while I stood outside next to his window.

My old way of dealing with a situation like this was based in fear. I would be repulsed by his behavior. I would be turned off by his insecurity, and I would either react with anger and make him wrong or be indifferent and eventually walk away from the relationship. But this time was different. This time, I held space for him to experience his emotions. I was loving and compassionate with him. As I stood outside his window, the sun was setting, and I could feel the warm rays on my face. I felt peaceful and grounded. He was inside his truck, covered by shade, sitting in the darkness, and I was standing in the light. It was a surreal moment for me.

In a calm voice, I asked, "Why are you choosing to feel this way?"

The first few times I asked him this, he raised his voice and said, "Why the f-ck do you think, Vanessa?

Because your f-cking ex-boyfriend is here."

I mustered up the courage to keep myself out of defense mode. "Can we try this again with more accountability?" I asked. "Why are *you choosing* to feel this way?"

Again, he went into the blame game, naming me as the cause of his negative feelings. The entire time he was going off and blaming me for his unhappiness, I kept holding loving space for him. In my head, I was singing *All You Need is Love* by the Beatles.

After five minutes or so, he calmed down, and I knew he was ready to listen. This was the point I reached out to him and reminded him that we're never upset for the reasons we think. He didn't say anything in response. I could tell he was still processing things, so I continued speaking from a place of love and compassion. I gently encouraged him to see a bigger picture by reminding him that there are many ways to look at a situation. We can always choose a more peaceful perspective.

His silence prompted me to continue speaking from a place of love. I softly explained other angles he could choose to look at the situation. As I was speaking, I could feel his energy lighten. I could feel him soften and shift into a new frame of mind.

He remained quiet as I stood outside his window. The sun continued to shine on me, and I felt peaceful, powerful, and confident. I was on solid ground, and nothing he could say or do would shake me. I felt the power of love.

After a few more minutes, I walked around and got into the passenger side of the car. Soon, we were engaged in an enjoyable conversation. The negative charge had been diffused, and by the end of the evening, we were spending time with his parents and back to loving each other again.

Transformation—this is what it means to be the change we wish to see in the world. I didn't need my partner to do anything differently. I didn't try to control him or make him wrong. I simply loved him. I held loving space for him to be accepted. I didn't let my fear get triggered. I didn't take things personally and get defensive. Instead, I focused on loving him from a powerful place of choosing a big-picture perspective. I didn't have any expectations. I didn't have a hidden agenda. I just loved him and saw into him through all his fear and insecurity. I chose to see the best in him and helped him see it too.

The only thing I changed was myself. I changed my attitude. I changed my approach. I changed my choices. I chose love. When I chose love, I could help *him* choose love, not by forcing it on him, but by showing him what it looks like and leading by example. I watched him shift from an ugly, angry, and fearful place to a gentle, loving, and peaceful place. I didn't *do* anything; I simply responded with love.

If I could choose any superpower or special ability, I would choose to *always* respond with love.

Before I became familiar with the MBT model, I remember being in deep meditation and asking Source,

Why are we here? If we're already perfect love, why do we need to experience all this? We aren't perfect, came the answer. *We have work to do and choices to make.*

At the time, this felt right to me, and I remember basking in the wisdom of the truth that resonated with every part of my being. That didn't last long, and a few days later, my analytical mind kept asking, *What kind of work? Why do we have to work? Shouldn't it come naturally?*

This is why my heart sang with joy when I was introduced to the MBT model. All my questions were finally being answered. They weren't based on dogma, faith, or belief. These answers were based in logic, research, and physics-based evidence. This model provided a framework to understand how everything works together. I'd always felt the truth and could feel my way through life well enough. But my intellect continued asking question after question. *Why? How? What?* Just having a feeling wasn't enough for me. I needed more answers. I needed it to make logical sense of everything to see the big picture clearly.

As the saying goes, "I'm a spirit having a human experience." Or as MBT would put it, "I'm an IUOC experiencing life through a human avatar." My human experience includes intellect. I needed to exercise my intellect and make logical sense of it all.

Now I understand that by choosing to respond with love, we're aligning with our purpose and lowering our collective entropy. MBT helped me to understand this concept, and it provided me with a practical method to apply it. By recognizing when I'm making it about myself, I can shift my attention away from my fear and focus on others while seeing the big picture.

Chapter 10: Belief is a Trap

I BLAME MY INABILITY TO have an out-of-body experience (OBE) on the belief trap.

When we're honest with ourselves, we may see that fear is the driving force behind most of our actions and decisions. Fear is what causes us to create beliefs. Rather than stay in the fear of the unknown, we make up a belief and pretend we know.

Think of a time you reacted negatively. Recall any feelings of injustice, disappointment, or anger. Can you trace it back to a fear of yours that's been tucked away, lurking under the surface, waiting to become triggered? If your fear gets triggered, do you blame it on others?

You're late for work, driving along in traffic, when someone cuts you off and slams on his brakes at a yellow light. You get upset and honk your horn at the driver in front of you. *What an idiot,* you think. Then the dialogue starts up. *Who the heck cuts someone off and stops at a yellow light?*

Has this ever happened to you? Maybe it's not traffic. Maybe it's the slow cashier at the grocery store, the rude teller at the bank, or the kid with no manners. Whatever may trigger you, notice the feeling behind the thoughts. Notice the subtle annoyance, the frustrated aggression, the casual indifference. Whatever it may be, simply notice it.

Awareness is the first step to change.

I was recently at another personal development course for work, and we had a few different exercises on Sunday morning. One exercise included singing a song in front of our accountability team (getting outside our comfort zone), and the other project was to create a vision board and explain it to the same team. Most teams consisted of seven people, but ours had one extra, making us the biggest team in the group. Everyone took a minute or two to share their song, and when my turn finally came and went, they all looked at me with expressions that said, *That was it?*

"Do you want me to add more?" I asked. "Should I try a new song?"

They encouraged me to try a new song, which I did, but ended up forgetting the words.

For the next project, I was the last to share my vision board. Since we had the biggest team in the group, all the other teams were finished except for us. As I was explaining the things on my board, I could see my team was incredibly distracted. No one was paying attention; they were all looking around the room at the other teams who'd finished. After a minute, I stopped explaining mid-sentence and said, "Okay, and that's it."

They looked back at me, but the attitude of the group was nothing if not dismissive. "Oh, great. Okay, thank you for sharing."

What happened next was interesting. I felt my fear of inadequacy come up in the form of disappointment and sadness. It was time for a break, so I immediately went into the washroom to give myself some alone time to process my feelings.

Whoa, I thought. *This fear of inadequacy is heavy. I didn't realize it was so prominent.*

I felt like I didn't matter and nothing I did that morning was good enough. I felt unloved, disappointed, and sad.

I've practiced enough to understand that this was all due to my fear of inadequacy, but in the moment, it was hard to shake off. I said some positive affirmations to myself and did my best to pull it together before I left the washroom, but it was a process. I didn't immediately pull myself out of my little perspective. I didn't immediately feel better upon realizing I was making it all about me. In fact, I was quite withdrawn for a few more hours that morning.

I didn't share what was going on with my group, although they noticed I was withdrawn, and they encouraged me to share. I opted not to. Instead, I stayed quiet and assured them I was just tired. Being in the fear of inadequacy isn't exactly energizing. It's more of a downer than anything. I chose not to share my fears with the group because a) I didn't want to fall apart in front of them; and b) I didn't want any of them to think I was blaming them for how I felt.

Looking back now, I can see that my choice to withdraw was based on fear. Fear of what they might think of me, fear of judgment, fear of not being liked, fear of rejection…lots of fear. I don't beat myself up for not sharing; I'm just recognizing the fear and being honest with myself. In the victim story, it's so easy to say, "I was vulnerable, and my team ignored me. I'll never trust them again." But this is the ego blaming others for how I feel rather than mustering up the courage to own my feelings of inadequacy. The truth is, if I were completely secure with myself, it wouldn't matter who liked my song or paid attention to me. The feeling of self-worth would never leave me.

The MBT model helped me to understand how imperative it is to own my fears and insecurities. I only wish I'd discovered this model earlier in life. I sometimes ask myself, *Why didn't I discover* My Big Toe *back in 2002 when it was first published?* I really could have used this model back when I was struggling with drug addiction and stuck in an abusive relationship. Now I realize that, although I was searching for answers back then, I wouldn't have resonated with this model. I wasn't ready. It's like the old saying goes, "When the student is ready, the teacher appears."

Drug addiction and an abusive relationship were valuable teaching experiences that shaped me into the person I am today. Like everything we experience, we're always given the opportunity to decide how to respond to every situation, person, place, or thing that comes into our lives.

We commonly view our existence in three ways:

1. Things happen *to* us.
2. Things happen *by* us.
3. Things happen *for* us.

Let's look at the implications of each perspective. Using my past experience with an abusive relationship, if I chose to see that part of my life as something that happened to me, I instantly become the victim. I would exclaim to my friends, "Why is this happening *to* me?" or "How could he do this *to* me?"

If I choose to see this in a more empowered way, it will look something like this: *Okay, I know my thoughts create my reality. So why have I created this?* I might say something like, "I created this experience *by* focusing on what I don't want." For those who believe in contracts (life paths we choose to incarnate into), I might say something like, "This was chosen *by* me to learn a valuable lesson."

When we choose to take responsibility for our experiences, we approach the situation from a much more powerful place.

Now let's try on the third perspective, "This is happening *for* me." This experience of falling in love with someone who has difficulty accepting himself and, in turn, puts down those who love him the most is happening *for* me so that I may learn to accept myself.

In the end, I was still able to love him from a distance while working on improving my own self-worth. If a partnership turns physically abusive, then it's time to walk away. In 2002, I hadn't grown my capacity to love. I couldn't be loving and compassionate in my relationship. I had a lot of fear and ego hidden away. Back then, I wasn't able to hear the truth.

But I was ready for pieces of the truth. That was when I was inspired by Dan Millman. I read *Way of the Peaceful Warrior* five times. I was also inspired by Don Miguel Ruiz. I had The Four Agreements posted up on my walls. This was also when I became fascinated with *Illusions* by Richard Bach and *The Celestine Prophecy* by James Redfield.

These books were pointing me in the right direction, the direction of love. However, I still didn't quite get it. Yes, I understood that we need to love each other and help one another out. I understood the difference between good and bad, right and wrong. But I couldn't make sense of it all. I asked myself, *Why does Joe Blow treat people like sh-t, but he seems to be happy and living in abundance? On the other hand, Jane Doe is a saint, and she seems to have the worst luck.*

I'd been told, "If you always do right, then nothing can go wrong." But this didn't seem to apply to Jane Doe. Things were always going wrong for her even when she kept doing right. I couldn't understand what the point was. All these different spiritual concepts and Eastern traditions sounded wonderful, but I didn't apply them. I wanted to be peaceful, loving, and kind, but I lacked the motivation to really embody those traits.

I was coming from a place of *but why*? Yes, I should love my neighbor, and yes, I should be a good person. But why? "Because the Bible says so" definitely didn't do it for me. "Because it feels right" didn't do it for me either. I needed to understand why. It needed to make logical sense to me. I could never make myself believe. MBT was a model that satiated my curiosity. It satisfied my left brain and helped set my right brain free.

I'm learning how to trust my intuition rather than dismiss it. I'm learning to feel my way through life rather than think my way through experiences. I must admit, I still live in my head at times, but I'm more aware of these instances and often catch myself and redirect the experience.

I'm moving away from the ego-driven life and toward a connected life. My self-perception is changing.

I'm no longer starring in my own movie; I'm a part of something greater than myself.

Chapter 11: MBT and Relationships

I'VE SPRINKLED IN EXAMPLES OF how I try to apply MBT in my relationship with my significant other, Dan, and because of the valuable lessons I've learned from this relationship, I decided to dedicate a whole chapter to this topic. This is an area where many people struggle—myself included, as I'm sure you've noticed.

As a result of the MBT model, I've also found that I'm able to recover faster from struggles and learn more quickly. I may need to repeat certain lessons a few times before moving on to the next, but that's just what happens when you're a slow learner. Bear with me while I bang my head into the same wall three or four times.

If you're anything like me and you find yourself having a lot of challenges with your relationships, please know you're not alone. I've even heard Tom Campbell express that he gets challenged in his relationship.

The people we're closest to are often the ones who challenge us the most. Our relationships create a safe space for us to show up exactly as we are with all our fear, ego, and beliefs fully intact for the other to see. We get to see our own insecurities, too, if we choose to be aware. Here's where the opportunity for growth comes into play. As we face our fears and do uncomfortable things, we gain courage. The more gracefully we navigate our way through these challenges, the greater our growth.

Throughout our relationship, I became more agitated around Dan. I was irritable towards him, and I was always annoyed by him. I would sometimes snap at him over something trivial.

"We need to address our relationship," I told him. "We should work on our relationship to resolve the root cause of the problem."

As I finished telling him about how I saw him showing up (yes, I still point the finger; I'm a work in progress), I turned my attention to myself. We were driving on a Sunday afternoon, heading out to the wilderness to enjoy some quality time together. Our conversation went something like this:

"I've been having a hard time appreciating you and finding love," I said. "Instead, I've been really irritable."

"Yeah," he replied. "I noticed. What's going on?"

"I think it's because you gave me an ultimatum and told me you couldn't be with me if I was going to start a working relationship with my ex-boyfriend, Jeff. When you said to me, 'It's either me or him,' I chose you. I ended my working relationship with someone you label as my ex-boyfriend, but I just see him as a friend."

He didn't say anything, but I could sense him starting to get triggered and his anger starting to rise.

"I feel like I'm starting to resent you for making me choose," I continued. "I'm not very conscious of what's happening, and I'm trying to understand where my feelings are coming from by addressing it and talking with you about it right now."

I could tell his anger had reached a boiling point. "If you want to be with him, you should just go be with him already."

"I can tell you over and over again that I don't want to be with him," I said, "but you'll never hear it until you let go of your fear of inadequacy and work on your jealousy issues."

"I know what will happen if you start working with him, Vanessa," he snapped back. "It will turn into late nights, phone calls every day, texting each other all day... You might as well just go be with him."

At this point, we pulled up to a gas station. As he got out of the truck and slammed his door, I could feel his anger raging. My own anger was coming up as well.

As Dan pumped the gas, I took some deep breaths and told myself, "Goose-frah-bah." I calmed down, and he got back into the car, still fuming and angry. He turned the truck around and headed back in the direction of our home. I asked him where he was going, and he proceeded to give me the silent treatment.

"How old are you?" I asked. "Really, are you seriously giving me the silent treatment?"

I laughed and made fun of him, unaware of my ego and totally forgetting all the principles in this book.

However, I reminded myself of my intention and attempted to mend the situation.

"Okay," I said. "I guess I need to validate how you're feeling. Since you won't share with me how you're feeling, I'll do my best to understand you based on what I know. You're upset right now because you're always trying to support me, but you feel like I don't appreciate you. You feel like, after everything you've done for me, I still want to be friends with Jeff. Even more so, I want to work with Jeff."

I looked over at him, and his demeanor shifted as he nodded in agreement.

"I can see your perspective, babe, and I'd like to invite you to see a bigger picture. I'd like to help you expand your vision so you're not stuck in your perspective where everything is about you and you can finally stop perpetuating this cycle of blame, anger, and resentment.

"I see that you're trying to change me. You're trying to control me and my actions, and it's not just this situation with Jeff. It just *appears* to be Jeff. Even if you manage to control this situation, you'll just go on to find other things that bother you, and you'll try to control those things too. I'm telling you it's futile to try and control your external environment. It's futile to try and change other people. The only thing you can change is yourself."

I sensed that he was still uncomfortable, but he was listening.

"The reason you're upset isn't because of Jeff," I told him. "It's not because of me. It's because you have a fear of inadequacy. You have a fear of abandonment and a fear of not being loved."

Most of us don't like to be called out on our fears. We work hard to keep them hidden away. How dare someone expose them? This was when I tried to soften the blow.

"It's okay, babe," I said. "I have a lot of fears too. We all have them, and what we're meant to do here is address our fears and let them go. But first, we have to be honest with ourselves and own our fears. We have to stop blaming our problems on everyone else and take ownership once and for all."

That helped Dan soften up, and I noticed his guard come down as I continued to express myself.

"I don't like it when you try to control me because my fear of inadequacy gets triggered and I start feeling like I'm not accepted for who I am. I know I'm a good person. I know my intentions are pure, and it feels like you don't see that in me."

At this point, I got emotional. In fact, I can feel the emotions rising while I type this. It's a fear of not being seen for who I am, not being heard, not being understood, not having a voice, and simply being lost. When I break it down, I can clearly see that it comes back to the fear of inadequacy. If I knew in my heart and soul that I was adequate and felt like I was good enough, if I beamed with personal power and an abundance of love, I wouldn't need anyone else to validate me. I wouldn't need to be seen or heard. I wouldn't need to be accepted by others; I would simply be at peace with who I am. If I fully accepted myself, I wouldn't seek external validation or acceptance.

How do I start accepting myself? How do I increase my personal power and transform my fear into love? When I became emotional, I noticed Dan look over at me for the first time since the conversation began.

I wiped a tear off my face.

"Like most others, I want to be loved and accepted for who I am," I told him. "When someone I love tries to control my actions, I immediately allow myself to become triggered. I realize that, if I didn't have a fear of inadequacy, I wouldn't be triggered. If I was one hundred percent secure with myself and who I am, I wouldn't react with annoyance or irritability. But this is where I'm at. This is who I am in this moment. Right now, I'm working through my fears and acknowledging they exist. I'm hoping we can work on our fears together in a constructive manner."

He was still silent, but I could feel the energy shifting from tense anger toward curiosity and openness. As I continued to speak from a place of inquiry and exploration rather than blame and accusation, the mood lightened, and our dynamic started to transform. It seemed that communicating from a place of honesty and self-introspection helped Dan get curious rather than stay furious.

When I became vulnerable and opened up to my fear, it changed his outlook on our conversation. We shifted from a place of friction to flow. We moved away from the darkness of fear and headed toward the light of love.

We ended up enjoying most of the afternoon. We had a picnic in the park and spent some quality time together. But this isn't to say everything was great and we didn't need to repeat, revise, and improve the process. Every relationship is an ongoing process we will continue to work on throughout our lives.

Through my relationships, I can discover all the fears I've dismissed, ignored, and hidden away throughout the years. Fear manifests regularly for me as annoyances, aggravations, anger, indifference, and impatience—among other negative emotions. But MBT provides me with a framework for dealing with them.

By allowing them to come to the surface, I can accept, embrace, welcome, and work through them.

On a practical level, let's see what this looks like.

My fear of inadequacy is triggered when my partner tries to control me. When this happens, I have two options: a) leave the relationship; or b) stay in the relationship.

I've wavered between these options, and it helps that I've experienced both sides of the spectrum in previous relationships. I've been with an extremely controlling partner, and I've been with a laid-back partner. The interesting part is, I ended both relationships, not because of control issues, but because I didn't feel as though my partner believed in me. I didn't feel accepted for who I was, and in the end, I didn't feel loved. *Interesting.* This realization encourages me to look at myself, the common denominator.

MBT explains that most of us don't fall in love; we fall in need. Our partners look to us to fulfill their needs, and we look to them to fulfill ours. Each of us is trying to get something from the other. This becomes an investment rather than a commitment to love. When you invest, you expect to receive something in return. Love is when you give without expecting anything in return. People sometimes refer to this as unconditional love. MBT describes this as simply love. A conditional love isn't love.

When we stop expecting people to behave a certain way and instead start accepting people as they are, our experiences become a lot more enjoyable. Most of us expect others to respond to life in ways similar to our own responses. When someone does something we can't relate to, we call them weird, strange, annoying, obnoxious, etc. We can't believe they would do that, and we make them wrong for their approach to life because their way is different from our way.

This becomes apparent in our relationships. We expect our partner to do certain things, and when they don't meet those expectations, we're disappointed with them. Relationships are so much easier when we can learn to accept people as they are rather than holding them up to our expectations.

One of the personal development companies I worked with teaches that it only takes one person to make a relationship work. I like this idea because it reminds me to be accountable for how I show up, and I constantly need to be reminded to be accountable in my relationship. However, this concept also tripped me up to the point where I took on too much responsibility for the relationship. I was always looking at myself and how I needed to improve, and I often failed to see that my partner also needed to do his part in the relationship to make it work.

The concept that "it only takes one person to make a relationship work" borders on the idea of co-dependency, which is a behavior I am familiar with from my own experience. My recommendation, if you're interested in learning more about co-dependency would be Melody Beattie's *Codependent No More* or Jackson Mackenzie's *Whole Again*.

Although MBE focuses on the big picture and how to deal with your fear, I encourage you to look for other resources to address the nuances. For the sake of this book, let's look more closely at moving through fears in relationships.

I discovered a shortcut, a strategy to help pull myself out of a negative emotion and begin the process of letting go of the fear. As we discussed earlier, it's quite simple. The only time I feel a negative emotion is when I make everything about myself, when I take things personally and make it about me. When I relinquish this habit, I set myself free. I no longer feel suffocated by the negative emotions.

Here's an example:

Once again, I felt distant with my partner. We hadn't seen each other much that week, and I hadn't felt motivated to help him in any way. This was when I knew I needed to acknowledge the problem. If I didn't, it would just get worse over time.

My partner came home from work, and after he settled in, I snapped at him for something trivial, and he snapped back. I calmed down and encouraged him to find peace as well. I told him we really needed to communicate. Our relationship was suffering. "Let's talk about this."

He was the stubborn, silent type, so I said, "Okay, I understand you're upset because you think I resent you for giving me an ultimatum, and you don't understand why it's so important for me to be friends with Jeff."

He nodded.

"I totally get your side," I told him. "I've heard it over and over. I'm trying to understand what happens to me when I react to your story. When I hear your perspective, I start thinking, *What the hell is wrong with this guy?*, and I tell myself a story. I start thinking, *Ugh, he's so insecure and jealous, he's such a victim, how did I attract a victim with insecurity issues as my partner?* This is where I go, and I'm trying not to go there anymore."

I was making it about myself, instead of holding space of compassionate understanding and unconditional love. I ended up taking it personally and making it all about me.

But when it's about me, I'm coming from fear. I need to make it about my partner and come from love.

This was his story. It had absolutely nothing to do with me.

I told Dan that I was aware of how I was showing up, but I wasn't confident I could be the type of person he needed in his life. I took ownership for how I was showing up, and at the time, that was all I had the capacity to do. I wasn't ready for a relationship with someone who had temper issues and a lot of insecurities. I told myself that relationships were difficult, and I should try harder to make it work, but a part of me also wanted a relationship that was energizing and uplifting, rather than draining and disheartening. I was confused.

I began writing this book when I was fully immersed in a dysfunctional relationship with Dan. However, when I learned we were pregnant for the second time, something felt different. This time, I was well aware of how dysfunctional our relationship was, and I was already edging my way out.

At the time, I was going in and out of depressive states, and it was hard for me to understand why. I referred to it as "biting off more than I could chew," and that was indeed the case. My intimate relationship was extremely challenging, and I kept telling myself I was strong enough to make it work.

When I was seven weeks pregnant, I flew to Los Angeles to attend a two-day workshop led by Tom Campbell. This event was held in L.A., where Tom was introducing new physics experiments with the potential to create a massive global paradigm shift. But at this historical event with the capacity to dramatically alter our worldview, all I could think about was my relationship with my boyfriend.

I flew in on a Thursday evening to stay with my favorite cousin, Tufue. Tufue is an actress, and her husband supports her and her family as she does her best to carve out a career for herself. She lived in Long Beach with her husband, Jeff, and their two young daughters, Catherine and Anna.

Over the next weekend, I observed my cousin's family dynamic. I watched Jeff prepare dinner for us the night I arrived so Tufue and I could catch up with each other. The next morning, I noticed my cousin sleeping in as Jeff woke the kids up early, made them breakfast, then got them ready to take the family out for the day.

As I observed what a loving family looked like, my jaw slowly dropped more and more. *Oh my goodness*, I thought. *Is this actually happening? Is this for real? Do men like this really exist? Are there seriously men out there who are thoughtful, kind, selfless, and considerate? This isn't some fairy tale. This is actually a thing that happens?*

Yes, it is. I watched it happen right before my eyes.

As I witnessed this miracle occur, I slowly started feeling resentful toward Dan. This would *never* happen in our home, not with my current partner, the previous one, or the one before that. It dawned on me that I'd been choosing men who were incapable of putting others first, men who had a small capacity to love, and men who harbored a large amount of fear. And I was about to have a child with another man who had difficulty accepting himself and others.

I was disappointed in myself, and the resentment I felt toward my partner reflected how I felt about myself. After all, no one can make me feel a certain way. If I didn't have any fear, I wouldn't have resentful feelings. But I was full of fear, and I had a lot of resentment!

That day, I attended the MBT L.A. event along with nearly 150 other participants. Tom went over each of his new experiments with us in detail, and my left brain did its best to keep up. The next day was much more palatable. We focused on the practical side of MBT, then Tom fielded questions from the audience.

I asked Tom about my relationship. "I don't get it," I said. "I'm making it about 'other.' I'm focusing on helping my partner, and I'm coming from love. But this relationship just isn't working."

"It only takes one to love," Tom replied. "But it takes two to make a relationship work."

That was the missing piece that I needed to hear! It only takes one to love, but *it takes two to make a relationship work.*

I was trying so hard to love my partner and see things from his perspective. I thought I could do all the work and make the relationship flourish, but *it takes two to make a relationship work.* Dan didn't have the capacity to see where I was coming from, and he was unable to contribute toward the relationship. We weren't a good fit. We both had a lot of fear and insecurities, and we continuously triggered each other.

Tom also suggested I look at my selection process. What criteria was I using to choose my partners? Was I looking for someone with a big capacity to love, or was my criteria needs-based, fueled by fear?

I realized my fear of inadequacy was the motivation behind my criteria for a relationship. I didn't think much of myself, so I didn't require much from a partner. I thought I wanted someone who had a big capacity to love, but I had no reference for what that actually looked like. This was why I was flabbergasted when I saw my cousin's husband.

When you've lived most of your life in a state of high entropy and dysfunction, it's difficult to break free from the inertia and carve out a new path in life. You must actively seek new ways of being and open up to receiving them when they appear.

I flew home after the workshop and ended my relationship with Dan. I wish I could say this was a graceful process and I radiated love and compassion through it all, but I'd be lying. I was anything but graceful. Instead, I had fear popping up left, right, and center. My fear showed up as anger, resentment, disappointment, and grief. I left the relationship by yelling at my partner, kicking him in the shins, and slamming the door on my way out.

Tom calls me dramatic. I have no idea why!

Relationships are the essence of life. We're here to learn how to relate to one another. According to MBT, we started out as one monolithic consciousness needing to advance our evolution, so we individuated ourselves to interact. It's through this interaction that we learn and grow. We tend to interact the most with our significant other. This is usually the first person we see when we wake up and the last person we see when we go to sleep. In our culture, our significant other is the person we grow old with, and in most cases, this is the person we will spend most of our time with. Who we choose to be in a significant partner relationship with is important.

Chapter 12: The Paranormal

According to MBT, when you understand the Big Picture, the paranormal becomes normal and the supernatural is just natural. The more you have access to abilities that seem paranormal, the less you tend to use them. You realize that most things are better left as they are.

Growing up, I was always interested in learning about the supernatural. When my second relationship ended around the age of twenty-three, I had a five-year streak of being single. This was in the early 2000s when online dating was becoming more popular. I dabbled in and out of online dating, and when I went on dates, I would always ask my date, "If you had three wishes, what would they be?"

You can tell a lot about a person based on how they answer this question.

Most of the guys would say unlimited money, travel, health, or some other response that would become our new topic of conversation. If they asked me what my three wishes were, I would reply with, "To be able to remote view any time or place, quantum leap, and become invisible at will." This would strike up an interesting conversation, but I never met anyone who said, "Oh, I can do that."

When my husband and I divorced in 2015, I started dating again. I met my ex-boyfriend, Jeff, online, and our first date was at a coffee shop.

He told me where he was going the following month, a facility where they taught courses on remote viewing, astral projection, and lucid dreaming.

"*Say what?*" I asked.

"Yeah," he said in a quiet voice. I'm guessing he was worried others would hear him and think he was crazy. "I'm taking a course with a physicist who's been astral projecting for years, and he's done so in a very scientific way."

By that point, my jaw was on the floor. "Shut the front door!"

Jeff went on to introduce me to My Big Toe and the Monroe Institute. I was flabbergasted and enthralled. I could barely keep myself contained. Bursting with questions and eager to learn more, we went on talking for hours. When he asked me if I'd like to go for a walk, I declined but invited him to get together again soon. I fumbled for my keys, jumped in my car, then sped all the way home. At this point in my life, I hadn't thought about astral projection in years. I'd practiced a few times in the past, but I'd quickly given up without any success. To now find out that there was an actual place where they teach this stuff was mind-blowing. All I could think about was how to get there!

I pulled up to my house, ran inside, then went into my room and searched "out-of-body experience." I was determined to have an OBE (out-of-body experience). *I'm totally ready for it now*, I told myself. I was motivated to have an OBE because I wanted to experience more than this physical reality. I wanted firsthand experience of a bigger picture.

I found a guided meditation to help induce an OBE, lay down, and listened to the meditation. Nothing.

Absolutely nothing.

I just need to practice, I told myself. *It will happen.*

But it never happened.

Later that day, I looked up the Monroe Institute and found an OBE course led by William Bullham. It was full, but there was a waiting list. I put my name on the list and forgot about it.

A few months later, I received an email from the Monroe Institute informing me that a spot had opened and I was welcome to join the program scheduled to start the following week. Off I went, ready to explore out-of-body states. Before I had the vocabulary for it, I referred to this ability as "quantum leaping." It was one of my three wishes, but I never thought it would come true.

The OBE course was thrilling. All the participants who showed up had been having OBEs for most of their lives and wanted to understand them. Me and one other participant who was in his late seventies were the only two who had never experienced an OBE. We were the only two out of a group of twenty-four who'd specifically come to learn how to have an OBE.

The entire six days we were there, I listened to incredible experiences from the participants, but the furthest I got was feeling my astral arm move out of my physical body. When I felt this sensation, my mind immediately got excited. *O.M.G.!* I thought. *It's happening. It's finally happening!*

And then, *whoomp*, my astral arm slammed back into my physical body. *What?* I thought. *No…*

My wish didn't come true, but it came close.

After attending my first OBE course, I went back to the Monroe Institute a few months later for one of Tom's courses. The following year, when I attended the Monroe Institute for the third time, I left with some enthusiasm and excitement. It's always fun to hang out with soul travelers and truth seekers. But nothing paranormal ever happens to me—no out-of-body experiences, no multi-dimensional travel. Nada, zip, zilch. I mean, sure, I was overwhelmed with love and felt like I was connected to the larger consciousness system, but I experience that in my everyday life whenever I need it. What I'd envisioned was astral projection, visiting alternate realities and exploring the larger consciousness system. But I didn't *see* anything. Maybe Tom is right. Maybe my expectations get in the way. Maybe I expect an out-of-body to look a certain way—bright colors, tunnels, fairies, and whatever else. But when nothing exceptional like this happens, I tend to give up. Maybe I'm just not supposed to have out-of-body experiences in this lifetime.

Whatever the case, I'm attached to the data stream that gives me the information for this virtual reality. It could be that my intent isn't strong enough when I ask for LCS to give me a new data stream. Or maybe I do have a strong intent, but LCS doesn't *want* to give me a new data stream because I'm better off without it. If I were to experience other reality frames, I would probably spend a lot of time traveling to other dimensions and exploring the LCS. Maybe I'm locked out for good reason. *Or maybe that's the story I tell myself because I can't friggin' do it.* Who knows?

What I do know is that I'm experiencing this VR and there's no escaping it. I'm firmly grounded in this reality, and I get to experience all the amazing things here. As much as I want to explore other realities and meet new entities, I also recognize all the incredible people, places, and experiences available in this reality.

When I first journeyed into plant medicine, I saw multiple dimensions at one point. I remember thinking, *Whoa, there must be so much more!*

Immediately, I heard a voice that said, *What more do you want?* This reminded me to appreciate what's right in front of me.

Although I haven't experienced any significant paranormal phenomena, I do feel connected to something that I can't quite articulate. MBT refers to this something as the larger consciousness system, LCS. I really like the MBT model, but I realize it's just a model and what's important is what works best for me. After many years of exploring the MBT model, I realize what works best for me is the trust I'm cultivating within myself.

As I mentioned previously, I've always had a strong sense of what feels right, but my logical mind could never make sense of it. After a lifetime of searching, I finally feel like I can make sense of reality. I feel like I understand the big picture. Once I could wrap my mind around the big picture, it set me free to focus on what's right in front of me in our shared reality here on planet Earth. My pursuit for the paranormal has subsided, and instead, I'm more interested in connecting with people, learning about others, and finding interesting ways I can contribute toward the evolution of humanity.

Chapter 13: Non-Player Characters

THE SIMPLEST WAY TO DESCRIBE a non-player character is to call it an angel. I realize angels come with a lot of connotations, but that's basically what NPCs are, minus the halo and wings. MBT describes an NPC to be an avatar played by the larger consciousness system rather than an individuated unit of consciousness.

Tom often gives the example of a child who falls down a well. No one is around to find this child; the closest home is over a mile away. The child is stuck at the bottom of the well without anyone nearby to help her. She's crying and screaming for help when, out of nowhere, a man appears at the lip of the well. "Everything is going to be okay," he says. "Grab a hold of this rope."

The child manages to hold onto the rope, and the man pulls her out of the well. "Thank you so much!" she says. She hugs the man and runs home.

The child's parents are surprised to see her stumble in through the front door, dirty and disheveled. "Mom, Dad, I fell down the well," she says, still panicking.

"What?" her parents exclaim. "How did you get out?"

The child says, "A man came and threw down a rope for me to escape."

"Who was this man?" the parents ask.

"I don't know," says the child. "I've never seen him before." And she never will because that man was an NPC.

Non-Player Characters show up in this reality to assist and help us along on our journey. This type of phenomena is easily accomplished in a digital information system. It's not nearly as paranormal or magical as it may seem. Anything can happen in a digital information system.

For the most part, events that occur in this reality frame must follow the parameters indicated by the ruleset. There are always exceptions to the rules. As long as there is enough uncertainty, the LCS can assist in ways that help consciousness evolve through this virtual reality.

With the example above, there's a lot of uncertainty involved because there was no one around to observe the NPC come into this reality. There was no evidence left behind to trace the event back to an NPC. For all we know, it was a random stranger who helped a child out of a well. This isn't likely to cause a stir in this reality frame, and the results of the LCS intervening are more helpful than harmful.

My third trip to the Monroe Institute was for another MBT Immersive program with Tom Campbell as our personal guide and coach for six days. This would be my second intensive program with him and my fifth time at one of his events.

Those six days were a lot of fun. I connected with some amazing people, and we started an MBT support group team that would later meet and merge with another group of people who were interested in helping Tom carry out and document his physics experiments. The original group formed at the MBT L.A. event, and in 2017, and the two combined to create the MBT Support Group in 2018.

After that third trip, I left the Monroe Institute at five in the morning to catch my flight home. At a connecting stop in Virginia, I took the shuttle to the airport with another truth seeker named Nathan. We arrived at the airport, checked in, then walked over to the gates together.

"Do you want to grab a quick bite to eat before our flights?" I asked.

"Sure," he said, and after we grabbed some food, I suggested we go sit up at the bar. Nathan agreed, and we headed over toward the bar.

We were immersed in a great conversation as we walked over and to the barstools, but the moment I sat down, I heard a voice ask, "Hey, how's it going?"

I looked up to my right, and there stood an average-looking man who looked like he was in his mid-thirties.

"Uh, I'm good," I said, a bit caught off-guard. "How are you?" This man came out of nowhere, and he'd interrupted my and Nathan's conversation.

"I'm good, thanks," the man said. Then he ordered a Caesar from the bartender.

I turned back to Nathan. "Sorry, what were you saying?"

"So," the man said, interrupting us again, "where are you coming from?"

I looked at Nathan and smiled, then looked back at the man and I told him I'm from Vancouver and that Nathan's from Arizona. I asked the man where he was from, and he said Philadelphia.

"What brings you to Virginia?" I asked, trying to be polite. "Work," he said.

"Oh, yeah? What do you do for work?"

He pointed to a billboard on the wall behind me. "I work for that company."

I turned and read the billboard, which said something along the lines of, "Helping non-profits share their message."

"Oh, wow," I said. "I recently started a non-profit. Can I get your card?"

"Sure." He patted himself down, as if looking for where he might have put his cards. "Darn," he said. "I must be all out. So what is it that you do, or what do you hope to do?"

In a playful tone, I replied, "I want to change the world!"

The stranger suddenly looked at me intensely. "You can. You have so much potential. All you need to do is decide what you want and go do it. Articulate it clearly and move forward; give it direction. It will happen for you. If you deserve it and you work hard, it will happen."

I was bewildered and taken aback. I had no idea who the heck this guy was, and he spoke to me as if he he'd known me for years.

Surprised and amazed, I said to him, "Uh, thanks. Who are you anyway?" The man just chuckled. "So, where are you guys coming from?

I looked at Nathan then back at the man. "We're coming from the Monroe Institute where we learned from Tom Campbell, a physicist who created a Theory of Everything."

The man at the bar nodded.

"In Tom's model," I continued, "he describes our bodies as avatars that we play and make choices through. He also shares that not all the avatars here have players. Sometimes, the Source plays avatars. Tom calls these avatars NPCs or non-player characters."

I looked at the man. "I think you're a non-player character." The man smiled.

I rose from the stool and told Nathan and the man I needed to leave because my flight was boarding. I gave Nathan a hug goodbye and told him to keep in touch. Then I smiled again at the strange man and said, "Good talking to you. Thanks for the advice, NPC!"

He smiled back at me, and I never saw him again. I returned home to Vancouver, and he returned home to Source—a.k.a., Philadelphia.

NPC's can show up in your life when you least expect it. They appear in your reality to give you information that will help you grow and evolve because the evolution of consciousness is the purpose for our existence.

Chapter 14: Stuff Happens

Stuff happens, and we get to deal with it. What's important is how we deal with it, not the stuff that happens.

When all is said and done, this is the message of MBT. This is the meaning of life. Stuff happens, and we get to deal with it. Life is fluid, constantly flowing before us, within us, around us, and through us. It's always moving; it's never static. How we choose to dance with life is what determines the evolution of our consciousness.

When my husband and I separated in July 2015, I immediately jumped into a new relationship before the ink had even dried on our separation agreement. I was committed to my new partner for six months before I realized it was smarter for us to transition our relationship into a friendship. A couple weeks passed by, then I met someone new, and found myself in yet another committed relationship. This lasted nine months before I "woke up" and understood that I'll never be happy in a relationship until I'm happy with myself.

In November 2016, I made a commitment to be in a relationship with myself. I decided to take one year to focus on accepting myself, and this turned out to be the best decision I ever made. In that twelve-month period, I managed to completely walk away from my business in financial services, and I started a new career. I absolutely *love* teaching leadership and development skills to indigenous communities across British Columbia. I focused my energy on a non-profit organization that has grown beyond belief, sharing free resources (courses, support groups and one-on-one connections) grounded in purpose, clarity, and love. We've since launched a youth program, and we have over a dozen groups running weekly throughout five different cities and across three countries. In 2017, we became a registered charity. Most of our work depends entirely on the kindness and heart of our amazing volunteers. Everyone in our community gives back because they *want* to help. They want to make a difference, and they are.

But despite all this, my most important achievement is my kids seeing their mother leading by example. I'm showing them what it looks like to live a meaningful life, create a positive impact, and be one hundred percent authentic. (Okay, ninety percent. I still use a "phone voice" occasionally.)

In that twelve-month timeframe, I left the world of finance, entered the non-profit realm, and became a minimalist. I often wonder how my kids interpret the contrast between me and their father. I moved into a small, two-bedroom suite, and I drive a 1995 Toyota Corolla, while their dad lives in a huge, five-thousand-square-foot home and drives a brand-new BMW.

One afternoon, when my daughter, Nala, was five years old, we were spending some quality time together. "Mommy," she said, "why does Daddy have a big house and you have a small house?"

I smiled. "Because Daddy makes big money, so he has a big house. Mommy is starting over, and she makes little money, so she has a little house."

Nala nodded as she pondered this. I wondered what she was thinking and how she was processing the information. After a few moments of silence, I picked her up, put her on my lap, and said, "Baby, it's not how much money you make that's important. What's important is how you treat other people. What's important is *who* you are, how good of a person you are."

When Nala heard this, she leaned in and said, "I love you, Mommy." I felt the love as we cuddled together in our cozy little home.

Some time later, I took a contract to teach a leadership program in Lax Kw'alaams. I agreed to stay on the native reserve for twelve days at a time, only seeing my kids every second weekend. I felt guilty for being away from my kids for so long, but a video call with Nala encouraged me. My daughter answered the call, happy as can be, and we chatted for a bit.

"How was your day, Mommy?" she asked me. I told her I had a good day at work.

"Mommy," she said, "your work is more important than Daddy's." I laughed and said, "Baby, everybody's work is important."

When we got off the phone, I smiled, reflecting upon how my daughter came to that conclusion. Yes, I'm a busy mom with a clear mission, and I work a lot. I sometimes worry that I'm not spending enough time with my kids. But it's moments like these that help me to understand that the best mother I can be is one who leads by example.

I'm proud of the mother I am. I'm not a traditional mom, but I am me, authentic and true. I stand behind the values I teach, and I don't simply tell my kids how important it is to treat others with respect, compassion, and kindness; I *show* them what it looks like to embody these values. This is courageously leading by example.

Stuff happens, and we get to deal with it. Work contracts take us away from our family, and we deal with it. Writing a book takes us away from our family, and we deal with it.

I started writing this book in 2016. It's been with me through a lot of different chapters, and I've done my best to illustrate these varied experiences and the underlying theme of MBT. This book idea sat on my shelf for nearly a year without any activity. I felt like I had too many distractions to really sit down and focus on the book, so I performed a

Google search for "writer's cabin in the woods," or something along those lines. I thought that if I could run away to a cabin in the woods for one week, I would be able to direct all my focus into writing this book.

My search led me to discover The Banff Center for the Arts and Creativity. They happened to have a writer's conference coming up in the fall, and I happened to have an opening in my schedule during the exact same time of the conference. So, I applied.

I was apprehensive about applying for the conference because it was two full weeks, and I didn't want to be away from my kids for that long. *If I get in,* I told myself, *it was meant to be. If I don't get in, it wasn't meant to be.* To my surprise, they liked my work, and I was accepted into the program. So, there I was, surrounded by intellectuals, screenplay authors, published novelists, and highly intelligent people who were all working on their own pieces.

I applied for this conference about three months ago, and over the course of the next three months, a lot changed in my personal life. Most significantly, I decided to move out of my basement suite and into a house.

I found a house for me and my family to move into, but the move date was scheduled for the exact time of the writing conference. Before I left, I moved all the things from my basement suite into my kids' father's house, and I stayed there with them for two weeks. My kids and I were super happy to have so much time together before I left. Co-parenting normally limits our time together to four days a week; this was an opportunity to be together for all seven.

During our first day together, I was playing with my daughter, singing, dancing, and being goofy. Nala and I start laughed and rolled around on the floor, exhausted from all the dancing and jumping around like lunatics. I gave Nala a big hug and said, "Oh, baby, I'm so happy you're my daughter."

Nala smiled and said, "I'm so happy you're living with us for two weeks."

If this had happened a year ago, I probably would have cried and felt like a guilty mom for not being there for my kids. But I didn't cry, and I didn't feel inadequate. I simply hugged her back and said, "Me too, baby. Me too."

Consistently applying the principles in this book has helped me grow. The strategy I use the most is making it about others rather than focusing on myself. Stuff happens, and I do my best to deal with it in helpful ways that support others. By doing so, I feel good about myself as a by-product. It's a win-win situation.

Our two weeks together flew by, and they were a lot of fun. At six and eight years old, my kids still challenge me. They push my buttons, but I can see progress. The last day of our two weeks together, Nala and I were cuddling on the bed, and I felt overwhelmed with love. Nala likes to have "grown-up conversations." We often talk about my projects and what I'm working on. I was telling her about the writer's conference and my book, and when she asked me the title, I told her it would be called *My Journey Home*. (This was the original name of the book before I changed it to *My Big Ego*).

"Oh, that's a good name," she said. "What's it about?"

I paused for a moment and thought about how to explain it in a way that she would understand. To paraphrase Einstein, if you can't explain it to a five-year old, you don't know it well enough yourself.

"It's about learning why we're here and why we're alive," I told her. "Why we're alive?" She burst out laughing.

I laughed along with her and asked, "What's so funny, baby?" She just kept laughing. "Why we're alive?"

"Okay, now you're just being silly," I said, and I gave her a big hug. "Oh, baby, I'm so glad you're my daughter."

She smiled. "I'm so glad you're my mom." Then she paused for a moment. "You're a good mom." I teared up then hugged her so tight she started saying, "Mom, not so tight! Not so tight!"

Sorry, baby. I just love you so much!

If I were overcome with guilt and feeling bad about myself, I wouldn't have had the capacity to share quality time with my daughter. Instead, by choosing to deal with life in a positive way, I was able to create these special memories that will last a lifetime.

Stuff happens, and we get to deal with it. When people whine, complain, or don't follow through with their commitments, we get to choose how we respond: with love or fear. Love responds with patience and compassion. Fear reacts with anger and frustration.

When a random person cuts you off in traffic, you can respond with love or fear. Love takes a deep breath and empathizes with the driver who may be late for work. Fear makes us selfish and only concerned about ourselves. Instead of empathizing with the driver, we honk the horn and flip him the bird.

A friend talks about you behind your back. Love responds with kindness and understanding. Fear seeks revenge and harbors resentment.

Your spouse or significant other is dishonest and forgetful. Love responds with acceptance and peace.

Fear reacts with bitterness and anger.

All day, every day, stuff happens to everyone. How are we choosing to deal with it?

An important thing to point out is that love is not weak. Love does not put up with unacceptable behavior. Love is *powerful.*

Take the last example when a spouse or significant other is dishonest. Let's say your spouse is sleeping with other people and lying about it. Love doesn't just say, "That's okay. I love you, and therefore you can do whatever you want, including lying and cheating." In most cases, love says, "I accept you as a person, and I respect myself enough to walk away from this relationship."

Love is powerful. Fear is weak. Fear keeps us stuck in unhealthy relationships. Fear of being alone, fear of hurting someone, fear of letting people down, fear of making a mistake, fear of being unloved—so many fears. Don't let the ego try to disguise itself as love. Fear, not love, is always at the core of all our problems.

Too often, we're concerned with stuff happening to us, rather than focusing on how to deal with it.

Remember, you're never upset for the reasons you think. You're not upset that your kid won't listen to you when you ask him to put the dishes away. He isn't the problem. The problem is your negative reaction. Do you get upset, does it annoy you, or do you feel frustrated? All these reactions will make your life more difficult.

Let's look at the alternative to getting upset. You ask your child to put the dishes away, and he ignores you. You don't get upset. Instead, you get curious. You connect with him. You care about him, and you want to understand how he's feeling. Now, you have a lot more decisions available to you in your decision space.

When you were upset, you had a limited decision space that may only include a few choices such as doing the dishes yourself and complaining about your son. When you're not upset, you can sit down with him and try to connect. You can be silly and make a game out of it, you can do the dishes together, or you can even leave the dishes until tomorrow. More options become available when you're not focusing on the "problem." Wayne Dyer has a famous quote, "Change the way you look at things, and the things you look at change."[10] Rather than seeing your son as a defiant child who won't listen, choose to see him as a young child who needs your help and guidance. This is guaranteed to help you have more compassion.

About a month ago, I had the opportunity to host Tom and his wife, Pamela, in Vancouver for five days. This was an amazing experience. Sure, I've done lots of workshops and immersive programs with Tom, but hanging out with him was a completely different experience. I remember asking him if he ever got upset or yelled at his kids. Calmly, he replied, "Of course not. They're just kids."

This has stayed with me ever since. Now, when I get upset with my kids, I immediately think, *They're just kids.* It gives me patience and

---

[10] Dyer, Wayne W. *The Power Of Intention: Change The Way You Look At Things And The Things You Look At Will Change. Hay House UK*, 2004.

compassion for them. It also gives me a much bigger decision space and helps me be a better momma.

Stuff happens, and we get to deal with it. How we deal with it is what determines our evolution or devolution. Remember, it's never the *stuff* that really matters; it's how we choose to deal with it that matters most. We can't control a lot of the stuff that happens to us, but we can absolutely control how we choose to deal with it.

Chapter 15: The Mind Leads, and the Body Follows

Emotions come from the being level. Our body responds to who we are at the being level. If we have a strong, steady intent within consciousness that's rooted in our being, our body will follow suit. An example of this is the placebo effect.

If we're told a pill contains a potent substance that will alleviate our headache, taking it will often make our headache go away, even if the pill was just a sugar pill. It was the firm intent and the solid belief that made it so. The belief wasn't formed by an intellectualized thought. It may have started as a thought, but through repetition and focused intent, it became a strong feeling of certainty that came from the being level. This is what made it so.

The mind leads, and the body follows.

When I was pregnant with my son, I discovered a documentary called *Orgasmic Birth.* This film followed eleven mothers through their pregnancies and labor. Each woman experienced blissful, orgasmic births. There were a dozen experts featured in the film who explored how giving birth has become more of a medical procedure than a natural one. When labor can be experienced as a natural expression, it can be enjoyable and pleasant.

I can already hear the mothers reading this saying, "You have got to be sh-tting me. Giving birth is anything but enjoyable!"

I was ignorant with my first child. I didn't know what labor would be like, and fear of the unknown creeped into my experience. I was adamant about having a homebirth with my son, and against the disapproval of my husband and all my friends and family, I stayed true to my intuition. I delivered my healthy baby boy at home in the same bed we'd conceived him in.

My fear came up during the labor, and I did experience sensations I interpreted as pain. But regardless of the yelling and swearing, it was still a beautiful experience I enjoyed with my husband at the time, my mother, my granny, my sister-in law, and my brother, who waited in the spare room. We also had two midwives help us through the labor process, and after eight hours, the birth was a huge success.

A year later when I became pregnant with my daughter, I decided to really prepare myself for the birthing experience. I watched *Orgasmic Birth* five times, and I was committed to making this birth an enjoyable experience.

I was in Costco when I felt my first contraction. I immediately paid for my groceries, drove to our house, called the midwife, and waited for my husband and my midwife to arrive. As I waited, I felt the contractions come on. Every time I felt one, I would say to myself, "Yes, that feels good." I kept saying this over and over till it became a mantra. By the time my husband came home, and the midwife joined us, I was feeling really good! The mantra worked, and I remember shouting out loud how amazing it felt. Instead of an eight-hour labor like I experienced with my son, I had a ninety-minute sensual experience that resulted in multiple orgasms.

The mind leads, and the body follows.

Chapter 16: Intent Modifies Future Probability

Many of us are familiar with the Law of Attraction. The book and subsequent movie, *The Secret*, popularized this concept in 2006.

If you've never heard of the Law of Attraction, (LOA), it basically states that you are the creator of your reality. "Energy flows where attention goes." Whatever you continue to focus on will become your reality. For example, if you're always saying, "I'm broke" and "I can't afford this or that," the LOA insists you will continue to be broke because you're perpetuating a broke state of mind. On the other hand, if you're a happy, positive person who stays optimistic, you'll attract a lot of great opportunities. People will constantly say to you, "Wow, you're so lucky! Good things always happen to you." Your reality reflects your mind.

The LOA received a lot of criticism when it first hit the masses in 2006, mostly because the movie, *The Secret*, emphasized material wealth. I remember watching it alone in my apartment, and one of the people in the movie shared how he used to complain about being broke all the time. Then he started focusing on abundance, and all of a sudden, he started getting checks in the mail. It sounds too good to be true. Is it?

Today, the concept isn't as woo-woo as it sounded a decade ago. In fact, it's almost common knowledge. If you focus on something and you apply yourself, you will achieve it. Most of us can agree on this. But how does this work? What's the science behind this phenomenon?

A few years ago, I went to a workshop led by Joe Dispenza. Joe teaches a helpful meditation technique, and he does his best to explain how the LOA works on a scientific level. Joe explains that your thoughts send out an electrical signal into the unified field that connects everything. Joe's theory also suggests that our feelings send out a magnetic signal into that same unified field. When you couple your thoughts with your feelings, you send out a powerful electromagnetic signal that brings your desires into your reality.

For example, if you want to lose twenty pounds, you would think, *I want to release twenty pounds.* That thought will send out an electrical signal into the unified field, and now the universe knows what you want. The next step is to have a strong emotional reaction to the thought. If you want to lose twenty, you need to visualize yourself twenty lighter, and as you visualize yourself, you need to feel how amazing it is to be at this ideal weight. You see yourself making healthy choices and feel powerful and confident. These feelings will then send out a magnetic signal to the unified field, and it will attract this new reality into your world.

Try it out and see how it works for you. Lots of people swear by the power of creative visualization and the benefits of a focused meditative state. My ego is a little too stubborn for these strategies, and it led me to dig a little deeper into understanding the science behind the LOA.

John Archibald Wheeler was a legendary figure in physics. He coined the phrase "it from bit." In other words, all things physical are information.[11] Wheeler was one of the first prominent physicists to seriously propose that reality might not be a wholly physical phenomenon. He suggested that reality grows out of the act of observation and thus consciousness itself. Reality, by nature, is "participatory."

----

[11] Horgan, John. "Do Our Questions Create the World?" *Scientific American*, 6 Jun. 2018, blogs.scientificamerican.com/cross- check/do-our-questions-create-the-world/. Accessed 23 Mar. 2023.

Wheeler also noted that we first thought reality was made up of particles, then fields, but now we see it as information. Information theory isn't new. These concepts have been in play since the 1940s. Physicists are beginning to support this theory. Rather than seeing this as a far-out concept, it's gaining credibility among physicists.

How is this information-based reality rendered?

According to MBT, our reality is run on probability because that's efficient. The alternative is a deterministic reality with elementary particles from the ground up, which is extremely inefficient. Our reality is modeled and computed, not simply created with particles and atoms.

Reality is rendered by TBC, or "The Big Computer," which is a function within consciousness. TBC sends information to our IUOC, which interprets the information, and that interpretation then becomes our reality. Reality is rendered when needed or upon observation. There is a popular thought experiment that asks, "If a tree falls in the woods and no one is around to hear it, does it make a sound?" According to MBT, the answer is no. If no consciousness is around to hear the tree fall, then the tree doesn't exist. If you're into gaming, think of rendering much like *No Man's Sky*—on the fly. If you're not into gaming, let's break it down.

What is the database?

The database is similar to the concept of the Akashic records, a compendium of all universal events, thoughts, words, emotions, and intent ever to have occurred in the past, present, or future in terms of all entities and lifeforms, human and nonhuman. The database stores all information from the events of the past, including the things that could have occurred and the probability that they would have occurred. The database also includes future events that can occur, as well as the probability that they will occur. Through the database, we have an actualized past that shows us what did, in fact, occur. This becomes our history.

The "time is just an illusion" theory can pretty much be thrown out the window. Everything doesn't exist in the now. Things actually happened in the past, and things will happen in the future. Time is a necessity; we need time to grow and evolve. We can't make any distinctions without time. Time is real, my friends, so use it wisely! The database includes all this information, past and future.

I hid my past for a long time. I was embarrassed, and I had a lot of shame around it. I told myself that being a crystal meth addict wasn't something to be proud of.

In my previous business, people trusted me with their money. I ran a financial securities agency managing money for my clients, and I later recruited new associates and trained them to become financial advisers. How could I let anyone know about my past? What would they think of me if they knew the truth of who I once was? No one would trust me with their money. They would think I was going to steal their money and buy drugs with it. No one trusts a drug addict. Even though I left that lifestyle more than a decade ago, the feelings and shame that surrounded it still haunted me.

I left foster care when I was sixteen, and I moved out of my boyfriend's place when I was seventeen. By the time I turned eighteen, I lived in a trailer. This trailer was literally "on the wrong side of the tracks." It was tiny, had no heat, and rested in an old car yard that belonged to my mom's boyfriend. I lived there for a couple months until my mom's boyfriend kicked me out.

I managed to find some work and get my own apartment before I met Colin, the bad boy I fell in love with when I was twenty. Colin and I were young, dumb, and we thought we were in love. After a couple months of dating, we woke up one morning and decided to leave British Columbia. We planned to drive across the country in his Porsche 911 and live with his parents in Red Deer, Alberta to start a new life together.

On our way to Alberta, we stopped in Calgary for the Calgary Stampede, an annual rodeo exhibition that's known as the "greatest outdoor show on earth." We spent the whole day drinking at the beer garden before we found ourselves at a Snoop Dogg concert in the middle of Calgary. The rest is kind of a blur. I remember a few bits and pieces:

partying backstage with Snoop and chatting with his uncle, Colin's Porsche breaking down, some guys pulling over to help us, walking (lots of walking) and waking up beside Colin the next morning, not knowing where we were.

I turned to Colin. "Whoa, what happened last night?"

"You don't remember?" Colin asked, groggily but with excitement. "We sold the Porsche to those Lebanese guys on the side of the road."

It started coming back to me. "Oh, yeah. That's right. Oh my god, that was nuts!"

There we were, two young fools with no direction in life and a wad full of cash in hand. This was the beginning of an exciting new adventure. Within a week, we bought two tickets to travel the South Pacific with Samoa as our first stop.

We partied fast and hard in Samoa. For such a small group of islands, I have no idea how we managed to blow all the cash within a month of being there. We had barely enough money to move onto our next destination, New Zealand, or we could stay in Samoa and find jobs. We decided to stay in the islands and make Samoa our new home. Colin landed a job managing Salani Surf Resort, and I was hired as a media publication's distributor for Jason's Travel Media.

One evening, after eating dinner at the surf resort, we were hanging out at the resort bar. After a few drinks, Colin says, out loud in front of all the guests and staff, "You can take the girl out of the trailer park, but you can't take the trailer park out of the girl."

I remember feeling hurt and embarrassed. I looked at Colin and said, "I lived in a trailer."

Colin was apologetic. "Sorry, babe. It was just a joke. Remember, it's from that movie."

I always had this feeling that if anyone really knew my past, they would judge me and label me based on the things I've done rather than the person I've become. So I kept everything in the vault, and my past became my dirty little secret.

But by keeping my past a secret, I only contributed to my fear of inadequacy. Having shame around the things I've done is the same as having shame toward the person I've become. How can anyone grow into a strong, confident individual when they're tied down by the chains of their past? How do we move forward when we deny parts of our experience?

When we hang onto shame, we don't move forward. Instead, we stay stuck—stuck in self-doubt, stuck in uncertainty, and stuck in the shadows cast by our past. We remain in that darkness until we let go of the shame. By letting go of my own shame, I'm learning to accept all parts of myself, including my past. Openly sharing helps me to let go of my shame.

I had a lot of shame around my experience in Samoa.

Colin and I quickly became dysfunctional. When drinking wasn't enough to drown out the fear, we turned to drugs. First it was pills, and then it was crystal meth, otherwise known as ice. Crystal meth is a highly addictive drug that destroys lives. Colin and I had been addicted to ice for nearly six months before we became extremely paranoid to the point I became convinced that the whole island knew we were taking drugs and smoking meth.

We'd been on our crazy island adventure for two years when, one night, we were both high, and I shared my conspiracy theory with Colin. Even though my theory was far-flung, he was just as nervous as I was.

"How do you know?" he asked me.

"It's so obvious they all know!" I told him. "First, I crashed my motorbike, then you crashed your truck.

Yesterday, you wrote off the company car. We destroyed three vehicles in one week!" "Yeah, we had a run of bad luck," he said.

"No. We're meth heads, and everyone knows. The owners of the resort know too." Colin looked me worriedly. "How do the owners know? They live in California."

I glared at him, thinking, *What's wrong with this guy?* "How could he not know? Everybody knows. I guarantee people are calling them and telling them we're smoking crystal meth. We should just call them and tell them the truth."

Colin went pale. He started sweating and shaking. "Do you think we should?" "It's the only solution," I said. "We have to do it."

I called the owners, but they didn't answer. The phone just rang and rang. "No one's answering," I whispered to Colin. "Should I leave a message?" "Yeah," he whispered back. "Leave a message."

The answering machine came on, and my confidence started to fade. "Hi," I said timidly, "it's Vanessa from Salani Surf Resort. Uh, I just wanted to say..."

Then I started crying.

"I'm sorry we've been taking drugs. I'm so sorry we've been smoking ice...."

The owner's wife, who I'd met six months prior on her visit to the island, picked up the phone. "Vanessa, Vanessa? It's Stephanie."

"Hi, Stephanie," I said, still sobbing into the phone. "Colin and I have been smoking crystal meth. I'm so sorry."

"*What?*" Stephanie asked. "Are you serious?"

Apparently, no one knew we were meth heads. Not the owners, not our friends—no one except for our dealer. A week later, Colin lost his job and moved off the island. I stayed to pick up the pieces and find my way home again.

Our intent to sabotage our lives modified the future probability, and it became our reality.

When I was at the Monroe Institute in 2016, I sat down with Tom and his wife, Pamela, for lunch. "Finally, I have you all to myself," I said. Then I proceeded to ask Tom a series of questions that had been on my mind.

I learned more about Tom and Pamela, and I was charmed by their dynamic together. Tom loves Pamela unconditionally, and Pamela loves Tom in return. She takes good care of him, and he does the same for her. During lunch, I opened up to them and told them how I used to be addicted to drugs when I was younger. I told them it was a serious addiction and that I felt like it changed my brain chemistry. I felt vulnerable and scared as I shared this with them.

"I don't think that my brain is capable of producing as much serotonin as it should because of all the damage that my drug abuse did." My voice softened as I tried to hold back tears. "But consciousness leads, and the body follows."

With a nervous smile, I changed the topic so as not to make anyone uncomfortable.

Why do we feel uncomfortable when someone is vulnerable? Maybe it reminds us of our own feelings that we keep neatly tucked away. Maybe we fear the exposure of our own scary emotions. We have so many expressions when we see people being vulnerable: *pull yourself together, don't be such a mess, you're stronger than that, you're so emotional,* or as Tom would say, "You're dramatic."

Tom has reassured me that being dramatic is not negative. It's simply a way of expressing oneself. I'm learning to own my emotions and express them freely rather than drown them out with distractions. This is what it means to be authentic.

Keep in mind, there is a difference between being authentic and being a jerk. If you walk around angry or annoyed and you tell everyone *exactly* how you feel, sure, you're keeping it real and aligning with your truth. But you're also being a jerk. Walking around angry at everyone or frustrated with people doesn't help humanity move forward. It doesn't lower our entropy.

You don't need to hide your anger or frustration; that would be inauthentic. What's more productive is to feel those negative emotions and have a strong intent to shift into a bigger picture stemming from love.

This is an important concept to grasp because they are externally the same, but the external is not as important as the *intent* that shapes the external.

I remember driving in the car with my kids on a spring afternoon. It was after my son's soccer practice. He was seven at the time, and I took him to get a haircut afterward. On the drive home, my son started whining and complaining about his haircut. My five-year-old daughter was sitting beside him, and she started crying because my son wouldn't stop whining. Next, my son decided to hit his sister, and she cried even louder. This went on for a good five minutes before my son started screaming at the top of his lungs.

While this was all going on, I slowly felt my frustration turning into anger. I wanted to yell at the kids and tell them to *shut up*, but instead, I breathed, focused on their feelings, and made it about them. I shifted my perception and took my attention off of how I was feeling. I stopped thinking about how I wanted them to behave and put my attention on them, focusing on how *they* felt and how I could help *them*.

Rather than sliding into an old stimulus-and-response pattern, I chose to interrupt the pattern and respond with love. That's much easier said than done. This has been my intention for many years, and it's finally sinking into the being level. It took a while for this intellectual concept to fully integrate into who I really am at the core, but it was well worth the effort. The intention to be better, to improve who I am as a person, is slowly starting to manifest into my reality.

Rather than reacting to the kids, I chose to visualize my son's consciousness as a ball of white light, and I directed compassion and acceptance toward his consciousness. Guess what happened? He stopped screaming and calmed down, and my kids enjoyed the rest of the car ride home.

It's not about changing others. It all comes down to you and how you choose to respond to the situation.

We co-create our reality; we get to choose the movie we immerse ourselves in for a lifetime. What's the title of your movie? Some might unconsciously choose to experience hardship and pain, but once we know that we have the power to change the movie, we can put on *Happiness and Joy.* The characters may remain the same and the plot may shift a little, but the genre completely transforms from horror to inspiration, drama to comedy. As a result, everything feels lighter, and life becomes much more enjoyable. There's an almost magical connection between people, places, and events. The next time you find yourself in a car with whining kids, in an argument with your spouse, in a disagreement with your boss/colleague/friend, or in any type of situation you wish were different, just remember *you're* the director of your movie. What type of film are you choosing to produce?

Chapter 17: Dreams

If you want to know who you really are, pay attention to your dreams. How you show up in your dreams is the real, authentic you. Our dreams come straight from the being level. There's no acting or pretending to be anyone other than who you really are. We don't need to be civil in our dreams. We can show up to school naked, we can tell our in-laws how we really feel, and we can eat mountains of ice cream. All our true desires, fears, and feelings come out in our dreams. We are completely free of our ego. "May all your dreams come true" has a whole new meaning in this context.

To get in touch with your authentic self, have an intention to remember your dreams and look at how you show up in the dream state. Notice how congruent you are from waking reality to dreaming reality. The dream reality is another reality frame. This reality, however, does not have a strict ruleset and isn't often shared by other IUOCs.

For example, if you have a dream about your old high school crush, is that the "real" crush, or is it just your imagination placing your crush in your dream reality? The only way to know for sure would be to contact your crush and ask what they dreamed about last night. If you shared the same dream then, yes, it was the real crush. More likely, they would say, "I have no idea what I dreamed about," in which case, you wouldn't have any evidence to support that your crush did, in fact, share the dream reality with you.

Why do we dream?

According to MBT, the ruleset in the physical reality that we call the universe asserts that our biological bodies function optimally with seven to ten hours of sleep. This gives our bodies a chance to rest and reboot. The reason that the LCS has included this as part of the ruleset isn't completely certain, but we can speculate. Perhaps it gives our IUOCs an opportunity to learn in realities that are less constrained than this "physical VR." Learning in different realities allows us to make different choices, and this can help us to evolve. Sometimes, we get stuck on a problem, and it can be hard to solve the problem when we spend a lot of time focused on it. Dreams help us get away from the problem and come back with new eyes. This is why we often say, "I need to sleep on it." After a good night's sleep, we come back to the situation with a fresh perspective.

If you're one of the people who insist they don't have any fears, insecurities, or self-doubt, take a look at your dreams. What are you dreaming about? Maybe this will give you some insight into your fear. It has been said that dreams are the door to your subconscious mind, and now we know that the subconscious mind is the fear that we're too terrified to face. Step through the doorway and face your fears. Dreams are not an opportunity to check out. Dreams are an opportunity to make good decisions and grow up.

I've found dreams to be profound experiences that help me grow.

This morning, I wrote down my dream. I'll share the first scene and follow with my interpretation.

I was at a till paying for groceries. There was a mother and her two daughters next in line, standing beside me. I didn't want them to see all the money I had when I opened my wallet because I didn't want them to think I was wealthy. I was worried they would ask me for money or expect something from me.

When I interpret this dream, it's clear to me that I have a fear of taking on responsibility. I don't want people to place expectations on me, and therefore, I hide and play small. It's interesting how, in the dream, the people I wanted to hide from happened to be a mother and her daughters. The people who look up to me the most in my life are my mother and my daughter. And no, I don't want them to play small. I don't want my daughter to hide. I want her to live life to its fullest.

This dream shows me my fear of taking responsibility. Underneath this fear is the fear of not being good enough to handle my responsibilities and potentially letting people down. I recognize this fear, and I'm moving through it. Maybe I won't be able to handle the responsibilities, but I'll do the best I can. If anyone gets upset with me for not meeting their expectations, I won't feel bad because I'll know I did the best I could.

Dreams give us more opportunities to learn and grow. If you're feeling stuck and you want guidance or answers, you can set your intention to find solutions in your dream state. Or if you want to identify your fears, you can do so in your dreams by paying attention to how you show up. Dreams are not a time to check out. There is always more work to be done.

Chapter 18: Life is so Unfair

If we're connected through a larger consciousness system and our purpose is to grow, evolve, and support each other through the evolution of our consciousness, then why is life so unfair? Why do some of us suffer through horrendous atrocities? Why is there so much injustice in this world?

There's a lot of suffering in our shared reality. We look around and see millions living in poverty, others dying of starvation, war, crime, and destruction. There are a lot of horrible experiences. Bad things happen to seemingly good people. Life isn't fair.

Why would we choose to experience this world of injustice? Is it an evil trick LCS plays on us? After one lifetime, are our memories wiped so we forget how horrible this place was, and we unwittingly come back to experience it all over again?

Maybe when we're infants, we recognize where we are. We think, *Oh, no. Not this place again, Get me out of here!* But it's too late. We're already here playing the game, and before long, our memories of the big picture fade away, and we forget that we're even in a game. We become so immersed in this reality that we think this is all there is. We become out of touch with who we are, why we're here, and what we should do. We stumble around, lost in the dark.

Life is so unfair!

Some religions and philosophies tell us the purpose of life is to get off this wheel of reincarnation and finally reach liberation. They speak of liberation as freedom from this terrible existence.

MBT explains things a bit differently. In fact, MBT says we never escape! We're stuck here forever, folks. But it's not about being stuck; it's about being here to make choices that will help us evolve and advance our current level of consciousness. We continue to evolve. We never stop growing, and we continue to come back and help others evolve.

The more we evolve, the more we grow our capacity to love, and when we have a big capacity to love, we're no longer driven by fear, ruled by the ego, and only thinking about ourselves. With a big capacity to love, naturally, we want to help other people. We want to come back to this reality and assist others through their evolutionary journey. By helping one another evolve, we help the evolution of consciousness as a whole. We no longer consider life fair or unfair. Our goal is to help each other thrive and learn from one another. Our growth isn't aided by pontificating, preaching, or lecturing each other. Leading by example helps us grow together.

My mom, God bless her soul, was born in a tiny village called Moata'a on the island of Upolu, Samoa. My kids, myself, my ex, and our family call her Mama. Mama dropped out of school in fourth grade and helped raise her ten brothers and sisters.

Mama has an old school mentality; she parents through tough love. She raises her voice with my kids, and she smacks them on the butt and says *sasa muli* (Samoan for "slap your butt") a lot. In fact, it was the first Samoan phrase my kids learned to speak.

When I finished the work contract that took me away from my kids for twelve days at a time, I returned home and noticed my mom would yell at my kids or smack them on the butt quite often. I would take note, but I would never react. Mama raised me till I was fourteen, so it came as no surprise. However, I also knew that wasn't the way I wanted to raise my kids.

As I settled in again and the four of us started spending more time together, I noticed my mom didn't yell at the kids as much. She was making a serious effort to be more patient with them, and I didn't have to say a word to her. One day, after the kids left the dinner table, she started telling me about her plans with the kids for the following week.

I nodded. "That's great, Mama. Sounds like a fun week."

"Yup," she said. "And I'm getting better, Nessa. I'm not yelling at the kids as much, and I'm trying not to get so mad at them."

My heart warmed. "That's good, Mama," I replied, and then I took a moment of thoughtful pause. "That's really good, Mama."

How did my mom know to change? I didn't say a word to her about raising her voice with the kids or *sasa*'ing my babies *muli*'s (slapping my babies' butts). [12]

I'm far from being a model parent. I make mistakes every day, but my intent is strong. I focus hard on letting go of my fear and coming from love with my kids. As it turns out, my mom noticed, and now she is doing the same. Trying to control people and make them behave the way we want is counterproductive. It won't yield the results we hope for. The best way to help people grow is to lead by example. Walk the walk and talk the talk. We show others what it looks like to be an evolved being. Or in my case, we show others what it looks like to walk on the path of consciousness evolution. This brings us back to the original question: why is life unfair?

Fair according to what? According to the culture we've created throughout humanity according to the human condition?

Or according to the big picture?

Considering the big picture, we're all incarnating into this reality, over and over again, experiencing different lifetimes. We experience what it's like to be rich, poor, sick, healthy, fat, thin, male, female, tall, short, and everything in between. They are all different experiences, and they're all valuable.

As Tom says, "What makes you evolve is the quality of your choices. Not the stuff you have, not the stuff that happens to you. The only thing we deserve is an opportunity to make good choices, and we all have that."

---

[12] This is not proper Samoan. It's palagi (foreigner), broken Samoan.

Chapter 19: The Low Entropy Story

I SEE A WORLD FILLED with laughter, joy, and kindness. I see us as a humanity that cares for each other with compassion, empathy, and understanding. Rather than putting each other down, we lift each other up. Instead of approaching life with a *what's in it for me* mentality, we engage by asking, "How can I help?"

I see a balanced world where we share our resources and support each other in ways that result in no one going without, a world where everyone has enough. I see a just world where we all have homes to live in along with clean drinking water, healthy food, and kind friends to share our lives with. I see a world where we take care of our planet, our animals, and each other.

How will we create this new reality?

Rather than pointing the finger at each other and blaming one another for what's wrong in our world, we'll focus on being part of the solution. Or as Maya Angelou once said, "If you don't like something, change it. If you can't change it, change your attitude." [13] Groaning and moaning about what's wrong and condemning others for raising our entropy isn't the solution to creating a better world. Once we acknowledge what's not

[13] Angelou, Maya. (2014, May 28). *Maya Angelou: In her own words*. BBC News. Retrieved March 30, 2023, from www.bbc.com/news/world-us-canada-27610770.

working, we must take action to do what's right and make a positive contribution toward lowering our collective entropy.

The reason many of us blame our external world for our problems is because we have different parts of ourselves we don't acknowledge, parts we've relegated to the subconscious. In a sense, we've disowned these parts, and until we face them, they will continue to haunt us. What are these parts we've disowned? Insecurity, shame, guilt, rejection—anything that's too uncomfortable to face. But by building up the courage to face these parts, we become whole again. The same is true in the big picture. Once each of us accepts all parts of our individual selves, we accept all parts of ourselves as consciousness.

All IUOC's (people) matter. Just because one piece of our consciousness is fumbling its way through kindergarten doesn't make it less important than a piece of our consciousness that's graduated from high school. The same is true for our individual selves; all parts of us matter. If there are parts of ourselves we're not proud of, we can learn to have compassion and acceptance for them. Just as all people are important, all parts of us are important.

As within, so without. When we find parts of ourselves that we're not happy with, there's no need to shame ourselves or beat ourselves up. Instead, we can accept ourselves with empathy and understanding. It's through this acceptance that we learn and grow without feeling threatened, afraid, or guilty. When we feel safe, we open up and learn through self-reflection, feedback, and guidance. When we feel threatened or afraid, we get defensive and shut down.

When each of us takes responsibility for our own fears and insecurities, we no longer project our shortcomings onto others. Instead, we take ownership of these areas, and we do the work that's required to let go of our fear. As we remove our fear, we're left with love, resulting in more patience, compassion, and kindness for ourselves and others. This understanding helps us to see that change starts from within.

This is precisely what the Low Entropy Foundation organization stands for. We are a registered charity that makes personal development accessible to all by giving people tools and resources to positively change themselves and the world.

The year 2015 was a turning point in my life. I left my marriage and my business. It was the beginning of a new chapter. During this period, I had a lot of time for self-reflection. Throughout my life, I've always asked myself the same questions: *Why am I here? What's the purpose of my existence?* I realized I wasn't alone in my quest for truth, so I started a group to engage people in deep, meaningful discussions. I called the group Conscious Connections.

Within a year, we had multiple Conscious Connections groups in five cities. Several participants mentioned how they wished they had something like this when they were younger. As a result, we created a youth program. We recognized how crucial it was for our younger generation to feel empowered and confident, so we developed Youth Empowering Youth.

It was during this time, in 2017, that someone suggested I start a non-profit to help sustain these free programs. After self-education in social justice and public policy, I gathered a board of directors, and the Low Entropy Foundation was born. We strive to create a world that's kind, caring, compassionate, and empathetic toward all.

By 2020, the Conscious Connections sharing circles we started in 2015 and the youth program we started in 2017 grew to an international reach. These adult circles and youth programs became popular because those who were involved had a clear intention to create a kind, caring, compassionate space where everyone brought out the best in each other. Many folks had transformative experiences, me included. We found that when you surround yourself with good people who hold you in a positive light, you start to see yourself in a more positive light.

In April of 2020, I began a full-time career as the executive director of the Low Entropy Foundation. Since then, we've added many more free programs for seniors, children, youth, immigrants, and anyone seeking support and connection. Today, we help thousands of people across the globe by giving them opportunities to actualize their full potential. We do this in many ways, including education, employment, coaching, and supporting community members with food insecurity.

My Polynesian roots could have inspired one of our philosophies at Low Entropy. It's our belief that we are one big family, or *ohana*, and no one should be left behind. Because of this, our free programs are offered to anyone who needs them. An example of this is the Youth Empowering Youth Program, or Y.E.Y. We recognized many children and youth had difficulty connecting with and expressing their thoughts and feelings. In response to this, we created an expressive arts program that supports children in identifying and exploring their emotions in a safe environment. Another example is our seniors' program. We noticed many people from our older generation felt isolated and alone. Just Older Youth, or J.O.Y., was created to address this issue. We organize monthly, in-person events to engage with seniors and weekly virtual events to keep our aging population feeling connected and supported by the community.

We are a microcosm of what we hope to see reflected in the macrocosm. Our vision is to create a global humanity that takes care of one another. We hope to achieve this vision through our example and recognizing the work we each need to do to make this world a better place. This isn't to say that we don't have our challenges and opportunities for growth. It's a journey, and I acknowledge that we still have a long way to go. But I'm hopeful that we will create this new reality over the next forty years. I feel confident that we will leave our future generation with a world we can be proud of.

When we leave this life experience packet, we can reflect on the life we lived and humbly say that we left this reality better than we found it.

Chapter 20: Happily Ever After

On September 19th, 2021, I married the kindest, most caring man I've ever met. (No, not Tom. First, he's taken. And second, he's old enough to be my dad!) I married William, a compassionate and loving man. Our close friends and family were there with us to celebrate this special day.

At the end of our wedding reception, I thanked my friends and family for their continued love and support. I remember feeling overwhelmed with appreciation for all their love. My friends and family have witnessed my journey through dysfunctional relationships, and although they may not have agreed with a lot of my choices, they were always there for me. It was through their love that I began to accept myself. I remember thanking them for this and letting them know that it was because of them that I now get to live happily ever after.

I met William in 2019, and when I first met him, I thought he was a nice guy. I didn't experience fireworks and crazy chemistry like I did in the past. Instead, I experienced genuine connection and companionship. This was foreign to me, but I leaned in, wanting to see where it would go.

After slowly getting to know each other, our friendship grew into a beautiful, romantic bond. Rather than rushing into a relationship and forcing it to work, we took our time and allowed our connection to flourish. Over time, I began to feel the chemistry between us. But this time, it felt safe, secure, and sustainable. When I reflect on my previous relationships, I realize the chemistry came from a superficial space. It was as though I wanted it so bad that I distorted reality by only choosing to see what I wanted.

Today, I'm experiencing a love like no other. William cares about me, values me, and brings out the best in me. I do my best to reciprocate this to Will, and together, we've created a meaningful, love-based relationship. At times, it seems surreal. I went from experiencing previous relationships where my partners constantly blamed me and projected their unhealed trauma onto me, to experiencing a relationship where my partner encourages and supports me.

Will and I met through an online dating app. After texting and talking on the phone for a week, we decided to meet in person at a local coffee shop. After three months of dating, we had our first kiss, and from there, our chemistry grew stronger. We've been together for three years, and he's only ever treated me with compassion and respect. He's never raised his voice or said an unkind word to me.

So how did I do it? How did I finally break the pattern of dysfunctional relationships? I recognized that we're here to evolve and many of our toughest experiences teach us our biggest lessons. After my dysfunctional relationship with Dan, I took a break from relationships and focused on myself. Afterward, I felt ready to meet someone new, and I quickly repeated the same mistake again—only this time, the dysfunction was magnified by ten. I found myself in a trauma bond with someone who had narcissistic personality disorder. This turned out to be a nine-month whirlwind of a romance where I ended the relationship by hitting rock bottom and reaching emotional, spiritual, and physical exhaustion. This was the most toxic relationship I've ever experienced, and this relationship taught me the most about myself. The end of this relationship left me scrambling to understand what the heck just happened.

Because I recognized that we're here to evolve, I took this experience as a learning opportunity, and for the first time, I finally saw my codependent nature. This awareness motivated me to learn more about personality disorders, codependency, and toxic relationships. Through my learning, my understanding of relationships changed, and shortly after, I met Will.

When I read through this book and revisit my previous dysfunctional relationships, I'm filled with empathy for myself and my partners. This compassion extends to others who share similar struggles in relationships. When toxic, dysfunctional relationships are all you know, it's hard to imagine relationships being any other way. I can assure you that healthy, loving relationships are not only possible, but exactly what we're here to create. We're here to learn love, compassion, and kindness, and we learn these qualities through our relationships.

We exist in this reality to relate, interact, and engage with each other. Relationships provide us with opportunities for growth. Upon reflection on my romantic relationships, I see slow growth throughout this life experience packet. I've grown from a needs-based relationship to a love-based relationship. I've evolved from a relationship where my partner berates me to a relationship where my partner uplifts me.

In my relationship prior to Will, my partner wanted to be a father. I became pregnant with his child, we got engaged and shortly thereafter, I had a miscarriage. During one of his regular temper tantrums, he said to me, "If you don't get pregnant again, I'm leaving you." Clearly, he was in the relationship to get his needs met, and he thought he needed to be a father. I was in the relationship because I thought I needed to feel loved. We were both engaged in a needs-based relationship.

In my current relationship, my partner loves and accepts me exactly as I am. When Will and I were dating, I told him that I wanted to be a surrogate mother so I could help a couple have a family of their own. Will supported my decision, and last summer, he held my hand as I delivered baby Max into the world. Will wasn't thinking about what was in it for him. Instead, he asked, "How can I help?" Together, we've created a loved-based relationship.

This is the most rewarding area of my life. Now that I have this solid foundation in place, I get to share with others from this place of love.

I'm pregnant again as a surrogate mother, due to give Max a sibling this spring. I'm onto the next phase of life, moving from intellectualizing and philosophizing to practicing and applying.

At times, I barely recognize my previous life, alone with no friends, living out of my tent, and recovering from a crystal meth addiction. It's hard to believe I was once so lost. When I compare my past life to my current life—full-time working mother, happily married, and now a published author—I'm left in awe and wonder at the drastic contrast. I can clearly see how changing my view of reality has positively impacted my world.

With all these responsibilities, I still make time to volunteer with the MBT community. Once every three months, I facilitate a question-and-answer session with Tom and the volunteers who help make MBT more accessible to the public. I gain a lot of value and inspiration from these conversations, and I hope to continue being a part of this community for as long as they'll have me.

My hope is that everyone finds a model or philosophy that helps them to actualize their full potential and contribute toward building a kinder, caring, more compassionate world.

References and Notes

Chapter 2: MBT in a Nutshell

Feynman, Richard. "Nanotechnology: There's Plenty of Room at the Bottom." *Engineering and Science (Caltech Magazine)* Feb. 1960.

Muller, Andreas. "What Is Quantum Entanglement? A Physicist Explains Einstein's 'Spooky Action at a Distance'." *Astronomy,* 7 Oct. 2022, astronomy.com/news/2022/10/what-is-quantum-entanglement. Accessed 23 Mar. 2023.

Chapter 5: Why We Exist

William, Shakespeare. *As You Like It. Digireads.Com Publishing,* 2016.

Chapter 6: Ego

Tolle, Eckhart. *A New Earth: Awakening to Your Life's Purpose. Penguin,* 2008.

Campbell, Thomas. *My Big Toe: A Trilogy Unifying Philosophy, Physics, and Metaphysics: Awakening, Discovery, Inner Workings.* Lightning Strike Books, 2007.

"The best way to find yourself is to lose yourself in the service of others."—Define this quote by Mahatma Gandi." *eNotes Editorial,* 28 Feb. 2012, https://www.enotes.com/homework-help/the-best-way- to-find-yourself-is-to-lose-yourself-405335. Accessed 23 Mar. 2023.

Chapter 7: Love is Letting Go of Fear

The Collected Works of Mahatma Gandhi (Electronic Book). vol. 13, *Publications Division Government of India,* 1999.

Chapter 9: Fear Shrinks, Love Grows

Arnold, Carrie. "Why You're More Likely To Be Killed By a Bee Than a Bear." *National Geographic,* 10 Aug. 2015, www.nationalgeographic.com/animals/article/150810-grizzly-bears-attack-yellowstone-animals. Accessed 23 Mar. 2023.

Tolle, Eckhart. *A New Earth: Awakening to Your Life's Purpose.* Penguin, 2008.

Chapter 14: Stuff Happens

Dyer, Wayne W. *The Power Of Intention: Change The Way You Look At Things And The Things You Look At Will Change. Hay House UK,* 2004.

Chapter 16: Intent Modifies Future Probability

Horgan, John. "Do Our Questions Create the World?" *Scientific American,* 6 Jun. 2018, blogs.scientificamerican.com/cross-check/do-our-questions-create-the-world/. Accessed 23 Mar. 2023.

Chapter 19: The Low Entropy Story

Angelou, Maya. (2014, May 28). Maya Angelou: In her own words. BBC News. Retrieved March 30, 2023, from www.bbc.com/news/world-us-canada-27610770.

Acknowledgements

Throughout the years, Tom Campbell has shown me patience, kindness, and wisdom. Tom's wife, Pamela, has also helped me see the bigger picture by showing compassion. Thank you both. The love you have shown me has made this book possible.

Thank you, Noah and Nala, for all the amazing lessons you continue to teach me. You both inspire me more than you will ever know.

It is with great gratitude that I acknowledge Will, my loving husband. Because of your confidence in me, I was able to finish this book and make it a reality.

My parents are also to be thanked. Thank you, Mama, for always being there for Noah and Nala. I could not have written this book without your help taking care of my children. Thank you, Papa, for raising an independent, curious, and self-sufficient woman. You helped me find my way.

Thank you to my friend and talented graphic designer, Justin Snodgrass. Your encouragement and support helped me cross the finish line.

Finally, I would like to thank my publisher and editor, Hannah Kates. My sincere thanks go out to you for guiding me throughout the process, keeping me accountable, and cheering me on.

About the Author

Vanessa Wideski is the founder and executive director of Low Entropy, a social impact organization that makes personal development available to all by providing people with tools to change themselves and the world.

From high school dropout and homeless meth addict to world traveler and successful business owner, Vanessa has overcome many of life's adversities. Her diverse life experiences have helped her gain a significant amount of empathy and understanding, which she shares by creating various facilitated programs that help people find purpose, meaning, and direction in life.

Vanessa lives in Coquitlam, BC with her husband and their blended family of four children. She is a voracious learner, working closely with Tom Campbell, renowned physicist and author of *My Big Toe*.